VULGAR ERRORS/
FERAL SUBJECTS

Fran Lock

Out-Spoken Press
London

Published by Out-Spoken Press,
PO Box 78744,
London, N11 9FG

A CIP record for this title is available from the British Library.

First edition published 2023
ISBN: 978-1-7392652-8-1

Typeset in Adobe Caslon
Design by Patricia Ferguson
Printed and bound by Print Resources

Out-Spoken Press is supported using public funding by the National
Lottery through Arts Council England.

Supported using public funding by

**ARTS COUNCIL
ENGLAND**

Here is a list of incorrect things – The Fall

To the "feral subjects", with solidarity

CONTENTS

INTRODUCTION

The title of this book is a riff on Thomas Browne's *Pseudodoxia Epidemica* or *Enquiries into very many received tenets and commonly presumed truths*, also known simply as *Vulgar Errors* (1646). In this work, Browne seeks to challenge and refute the "vulgar" or common errors and superstitions of his age, including those relating to the fabulous, non-normative animal amalgams found within bestiary texts. Browne's three determinants for obtaining truth were the authority of past scholarly works, the act of reason (of which the common mass of man was felt to be insufficiently possessed), and empirical experience.

Vulgar Errors is a fascinating work. It is also an early and significant milestone in a long process of disenchantment, a project of collection, separation, and classification in line with the rationalising aims of the Enlightenment. There are multiple ways to characterise this process, but for myself the most persuasive is also the most uncomfortable: from mystery to spectacle, from spectacle to specimen. It is a project culminating in the museum, the gallery, and the zoo, by way of the Wunderkammer, the circus, and the freakshow.

I chose the title as a nod to the kinds of superstitions and myths that accrete around feral subjects, both human and non-human, but also as an invocation of their troubling and wonderful forms. What if "errors" were not something to be corrected? What if "errors" were the pannier-paths to a kind of radical freedom? These lyric essays have grown out of a consuming preoccupation with the imaginative yoking of abject animality and otherness. While doing my stint as Judith E. Wilson Poetry Fellow at Cambridge University I have been interrogating this connection between other and animal through the lens of the medieval bestiary, specifically the Cambridge University Library ('CUL') bestiary, a twelfth century Latin bestiary text, and later through a second (my favourite) bestiary included in a twelfth century encyclopaedia at the Parker Library, Corpus Christi College known as *The Peterborough Psalter and Bestiary*. My work at Cambridge has been focused on bestiary texts as poems of irrational anxiety; they create moral allegories by animalising non-normative or racialised subjects, and classifying their bodies as perverse, amorphous, or sinful. These bodies are uncanny and excessive. They are *feral*. From the CUL bestiary my reading crept ever outwards, provoking these interconnected, often tangential reflections on the literary and political treatment of human and non-human others throughout history.

Full disclosure: I cannot talk about the feral without raising my own demons, and while my time at Cambridge has been a strange kind of miracle, it has also provided me with ample opportunity to reflect on what it means to be and do feral. Feral has become the lens through which I think about and understand my relationship to my practice. *I* am a liminal animal, operating between and across stable categories of being and belonging, a glitch in the system. Any system. I am – as I have often been – 'matter out of place' (Mary Douglas, 1966). This is painful, but it is also joyous, motivating, and instructive.

Feral is the theme and the mode of this work, a teasing spoof on scholarship, and a burlesque of queer, working-class rage. It bears upon my status as a "Poundland Academic" within elite intellectual space. It performs what Stuart Hall and Judith Halberstam have called 'low theory': knowledge, eccentrically assembled and refusing to conform to the hierarchies that maintain the status and the functioning of 'high theory' (Judith Halberstam, 2011).

It is, amongst other things, vulgar, erratic, and over-the-top. It is simultaneously *too much* and *not enough*. It is libidinal and gamy, lacks rigour, consistency, authority, or "flow". I did that on purpose, you see? I would do it again. If you don't like it, you know what *you* can do.

— Fran

ABJECT SPECTACLE /
UNNATURAL LANGUAGE

don't talk to me about *nature*. feral is not nature. rather, feral is not *natural*. feral exceeds the natural. feral amplifies and distorts it. feral is disproportionate, the too-much idea of the animal; will surpass and cross. amalgam. of possible and impossible parts. a dubious chimera, a gaffed freak, a monster and a ghost. to be the mutant *and* the spectre, the *spectacle*, larger than life, less than material, fleshy and transparent. feral is something squeamish and tempting, glass eels swimming in thick, clear jelly.

+

spectacle. yes, as in 'hyper-visible filthy whites', defined by processes of racialisation, sexualisation, and by their lack of cultural adroitness (Imogen Tyler, 2008). at the reading a woman "compliments" my outfit as "brave". followed immediately by "*i* much prefer muted, *natural* colours." bitch please, have you *seen* nature lately? then, *sotto voce*, i am making "a *spectacle*" of myself. she is wrong. a *performance* isn't a *spectacle*, the performer does not *create* the spectacle, the beholder creates the spectacle. if *natural* is something the eye slides over, then *spectacle* is what? a moment of arrest and interruption. of malignant visibility, where the full weight of the beholder's stare is applied to the business of effortful annihilation. performance is 'representation without reproduction' (Peggy Phelan, 1993). performance is fleeting and fugitive; will privilege swerve and flicker, transition, strategic disappearance, opacity, and instability. to be the centre of the spectacle is to fall victim to your own public representations. in my cheap, landlady's leopard print, i become stuck, forced back into the ill-fitting-skin of aesthetic incompetence: ostentatious, artificial. something sluttish and crude.

to be *feral* is to exist at the centre of that spectacle. in a state of quantum uncertainty, simultaneously more and less than *natural*. feral is an unreliable receptacle even for otherness. the interval. the cut. feral dwells not in the objectifying gaze but precisely within that annihilating stare: reduced to fiction and to fever dream: reduced past point of fetish into flat 'inanimation' (Garland-Thomson, 1996). the feral subject doesn't have feelings, it – we – incite them. spectacle is the end of agency, of empathy. it is a closed circuit. we go round and around in the lockstep, lockjaw, goosestep of everything they think they know about us. i am not a self, but an inscription surface, the dead-end of spectacle.

+

'and your very flesh shall be a great poem...' says Whitman. yeah, on the subject of white fragility. directed by David Cronenberg. not feeling it today Walt, sorry. when the wound is the spectacle. see, wounding is a literal practice (police brutality; the dropping of bombs; the shooting of unarmed civilians; the rape, starvation, or slow poisoning of the poor) and a psychological tactic (the freight of fear that accretes around each instance of wounding). think about what it would mean for certain bodies – black bodies, brown bodies, queer bodies, gyp bodies, women's bodies – to pre-empt the wound. when the beholder's eye anticipates the wound in turning toward you. to live inside the uncanny temporality of the pre-wound, inside a violence and a damage that is always coming. those bodies that become a collectivised shorthand – a summoning – for and of this violence, this wound. that trick of the light that says: *you are not who violence happens to, you are where violence is from.* irish bodies. i do not want to write anymore.

+

what it means to be *traumatised i*s to exist in the aftermath of violence and in the path of coming violence simultaneously. queer bodies so missequenced. and queer bodies caught in uncanny oscillation between *affliction* and *bliss*. to live in proximity to pain entails an obsessive pursuit of joy. joy is not an expression of survival, but its necessary method. against the wound that is always coming. fight spectacle with spectacle. this too is feral.

+

poverty is spectacle. the poor. the feral poor. pathologically unwilling to consume, or enacting a kind of skewed decadence driven by an excessive participation in consumer culture that is, nevertheless, ill-adept or ignorant, not appropriately tasteful or refined. focus on the spectacle, create a theatre of cultural incompetence, construct marginality on grounds of "taste" and "style", then no one has to acknowledge the economic conditions that create a social underclass, let alone exclude that same underclass from educational opportunity and cultural access. clever. my brother is a dandy. of his hyper-maximal style he says: *stars are not on fire, they* are *fire. that's us too, if we were ever given chance to know it.*

+

or. consider those others who are persecuted and excluded to such an extent that they become 'disinherited' from 'the possibility of being human' (Georges Bataille, 1993). classes of humanity so thoroughly omitted from the usual processes of representation as to render them paradoxically class*less*. these, the feral, whom Bataille calls the abject. rather, the abject*ed*. that is, forced to bear the figural burden of abject and disgusting otherness, to become a repository for all the negative and antisocial aspects of neoliberal culture so that we might imagine ourselves redeemed: the problem is not the animal industrial complex, the problem is halal butchery. the problem is not the white supremacist logics of capitalism, the problem is a single group of destitute and socially unaware racists. the problem is not systemic misogyny, but the way in which "gypsies" treat women and girls. the problem is not our collective unsustainable consumption, but the excessive, incompetent consumption of "chavs" and "pikeys". abjecting the other allows us to normalise our own failures, our own scenes of moral abdication. otherness, being "othered", that's not about my feelings, dipshit. that's a structure of power.

+

abjection is an essential component of sovereignty, which must, as an imperative, constitute a portion of the population as moral and spiritual pariahs: 'represented from the outside with disgust as the dregs of the people, populace and gutter.' oppression must concentrate within its static, self-contained, highly individual form, whereas 'the oppressed are formed out of the amorphous and immense mass of the wretched population' (Bataille, 1993). undifferentiated, denied the unique individual considerability of personhood. grotesque animality has long been a staple in the extensive vocabulary of contempt applied to poor, racialised, and dissenting others. but for the rhetoric and logics of dehumanisation to work, we must first delegitimate the life and presence of the animal, stigmatise them as scavengers, invaders, vectors of disease, who 'wrongly trespass on human territory [...] since they do not belong in our space, we feel entitled to eliminate these so-called pests in the animal equivalent of ethnic cleansing' (Donaldson and Kymlicka, 2011). Donaldson refers to these savvy animal trespassers as 'liminal animals', animals which in some way transgress the limits of domesticity, regress or reject the status and identity of "tame". these animals encroach upon or threaten the hygienic separation humans believe they have

4

instituted between themselves and what they are pleased to call *nature*. the liminal animal is a species that lives among humans but that is not subordinated to human controls or decorums. such animals cannot be instrumentalised – as food or as labour – and they cannot be imaginatively colonised, they're not "cute", they won't lend themselves to Disneyfication, to being carted around as cultural freight, meaningful only in terms of the sensations and emotions they produce in the humans encountering them. these animals are opportunistic, synanthropic, scavenging. because humans tend to put animals into one of only two categories – domesticated or wild – non-domesticated animals who live in antagonistic or ambivalent proximity to humans are deemed out of place, figured as pests or as interlopers, as ciphers for contagion, incursion, swarm and threat. this is the logic of the cull, that figures those animal populations without instrumental value as dangerously "surplus". historically, this idea of the too much or the out of place animal has been weaponised as a pejorative against vulnerable others, including but not limited to: women, queers, the disabled, the mad, the racialised, those racialised by poverty (such as the irish), to refugees, and to GTR communities. in the treatment of these others *feral* comes to stand for those feelings, affects, and embodiments that exceed normative frameworks of recognition and acceptance.

+

in the thirteenth century latin poem, *vox clamantis*, John Gower evokes the voices of poor, marginalised and oppressed persons through the use of animal noises, characteristics, and transformation. *vox clamantis* is an estate satire that opens with a startling allegorical vision of social revolt, where peasants are transformed – literally – into wild animals, and london becomes a terrifying and bestial wasteland. Gower's poem is presented as a strange prophecy or therianthropic beast vision, it is also a burlesque of the 1381 peasants' rebellion: rebellious peasants are struck by the curse of god, morphing into pigs, dogs, and monstrous poultry. as their voices degrade into animal cacophony, they leave their cosy heaps of dung and descend upon london like a biblical plague. the title is well chosen — it comes from the Book of Isaiah, roughly, 'the voice of one crying in the wilderness: prepare ye the way of the lord, make his paths straight.' and in this proselytising vein, Gower's poetic persona is both stridently moralising and oddly prescient. the poem is framed as a prediction of the peasants' rebellion (although it was actually written afterwards), and Gower claims to record the complaints of the *vox populi*, to speak on behalf of "the people", to reform while embodying his very particular vision of its collective concerns and voice. the cry, in its various guises, is central to Gower's text, whether as articulate lament or feral howl. for Gower, the 'common people' speak – and cry – with one voice, they have the same needs, aims, and ambitions: social harmony brought into being through good governance (yeah, the top of everyone's wish list, that). the problem with society – the source of the cry – is that nobody is fulfilling his divinely ordained role: from ineffectual kings to worldly clergy; from supine nobility to lazy and feckless peasants. to speak as one – in god's name – is the medium through which discontent is expressed, but it's also a powerful force of social and spiritual cohesion; language is the instrument of redress and healing. so it's telling that the peasantry are the only ones singing off-key in this chorus. Gower excludes them from the mass of 'common people' and the category of humanity altogether by transforming their voices into discordant war whoops and animal grunts. he shuts them out (and up) of the *vox populi*, which is besieged by and cries out against them. as Sarah Novak writes, Gower believes 'in the power of language to repair the ills of society, to compose peace. however, just as god denies

wealth and freedom to the peasant class for the common good —
because someone must work the land — Gower deprives them of
language, which would prove too dangerous in their mouths.'
(Novak, 2013). of course. but if the animal howl of the poor points
to a wound that exceeds articulate language? what if the poor
are not merely beneath consideration, but beyond consolation?

+

the 'curse' renders literal the peasants' abject separation from
the mass of obedient, patient, and pious poor, and Gower's text
is both compelling and uniquely nauseating in this regard. the
poem acknowledges the prevailing attitudes towards the poor
held by their superiors, and the degrading treatment that results.
to that extent, Gower is sympathetic to some level of *reform,* but
he is only able to advocate for these decent poor through the
imaginative creation of a feral underclass. all peasants are equally
lowly and coarse, but the humble and suffering peasant is closer
to god, the rebellious peasant nearer not only to the beast, but
the wild, dangerous, and unpredictable animal. Bataille notes
that although association with the scummy, wretched masses is
forbidden to the sovereign subject, this same feral population
must remain as an ever-present cipher of disgust and fascination:
an ob/abject lesson that sustains and contours the oppressor's
sovereignty and self-rule. duh. Law and Order governments
need a criminal underclass. nobody is working to put themselves
out of business. but society needs its dropouts, pikeys, hoodies,
druggies, sluts, swarthy others, freaks, and queers for less tangible
reasons too: in order, for example, to constitute an ideal expression
of identity, to enact and reaffirm this identity against a mass of
abject, subaltern others; to maintain and propagate this identity
by fomenting and policing distinctions between citizen-subjects
and across communities until this strict division of identities

becomes naturalised as inevitable. stitched up proper. while the abject other disrupts and threatens social and political boundaries, they also function as a key component in the work of category maintenance: instructive human wrecks, they serve as a warning to the would-be deviant. more than this, the revulsion they excite and the exclusion that results, solidifies those categories as meaningful. *oi, gyppo!* while the feral poor may refuse their instrumentalisation and disturb the social order, their oppressors can recuperate their use value as symbolic and political tools: as bogeymen, folk devils, scapegoats. the abject survive in this form through culture. politically excluded and socially reviled, the myth of the other is told, retold, embellished, and embroidered through art and literature until it comes to replace those it purports to represent. until the woman at the reading looks directly at me and sees, not the person in front of her, but a loose constellation of tabloid tropes. until Gower's peasants are so self-evidently and irredeemably animal that no one has to acknowledge their suffering or answer for their grievances.

+

think about this: the subjects of Gower's divine curse are doubly monstrous. they regress first to the level of animals, but those animal forms are themselves subject to distortion, exceeding their known, stable parameters. chickens become vultures, dogs become wolves. the domesticated beast suddenly bites the hand that feeds it, runs wild, goes rogue. Gower's therianthropes are in violation of both natural law and social order. natural law and social order are, in fact, presented as synonymous. the poor have always been one rung below personhood; this inherent inferiority excused their relative lack of freedom, and justified their exploitation. but the pacified poor, like their animals, were at least fit to be harnessed as edible resources or as units of wiry labour. the rebellious poor turned the world upside down.

8

embedded in the way we use (deny and withhold) language are a whole host of assumptions about degrees of agency and sentience. the thing about Man™, is that Man™ is a domestic animal. that is, he frames himself as uniquely artificial: his signal qualities are language, artifice, and abstract thought. he is the animal that domesticated itself, if you like. this idea is what Donna Haraway refers to as the doctrine of 'human exceptionalism' (Haraway, 2008), and it has been used as a lever to deny, variously, sentience, soul, mind, language, self-consciousness, technology, morality etc., to both non-human subjects and to animalised humans, so that the meaningful, meaning-seeking body becomes mere flesh, ripe for exploitation. in *when species meet* one of Haraway's chief and most compelling contentions is that 'the philosophic and literary conceit that all we have is representations and no access to what animals think and feel is wrong'. it's an expedient position that justifies their death and suffering, every bit as contingent and socially created as Gower's notion that god created the peasants to labour and to struggle.

+

if a pet dog or a farm-reared pig is turned loose it will revert to its wild nature, that wild nature is somehow always dormant and contained within the domesticated beast. in pigs this has proven to be not merely a question of behaviour, but of epige-netics: an animal's phenotype (or physical form) is dictated by its genetic code, this genetic code will be expressed in different ways depending on environmental conditions. so, to cut a long story short, if a pig is born on a farm, shielded from predators, kept warm, purposely fattened on nutrient-rich food, the chemical profile and outward appearance of the pig will reflect this. it might show, for example, lower levels of testosterone, thus it will be largely sleek and hairless. but if a pig escapes, it finds itself in danger from predators, cold and nutrient-starved; this triggers the relevant chemical cascade, driving morphological changes conducive to its survival. a human being is supposed to be different. if domesticity is our defining trait, then there is no essential or *natural* self to return to. the feral human must degenerate instead into a different order of life entirely. *feral* is not humanity distorted, it is humanity cancelled. identification with the animal order is total.

+

this notion of the feral turns on both an excess of autonomy and an absolute lack of control. this feral is not amenable to rational argument, to emotional appeal, to persuasion or threat. its otherness can never be breached or surmounted, it is completely itself, resists all attempts at coercive recuperation. and yet, this feral is frighteningly disinhibited: wildly animated, incontinent, hysterical. the underclass is frightening because the usual inducements of civilisation can have no effect on a populace that has absented itself – or been forcibly absented – from that category. the underclass is frightening because it – they – we – will not or cannot govern ourselves, yet we cannot or will not be endured by a society that demands passive compliance as its sole metric of citizenship. Kristeva describes the abject as 'that which is cast out' (Kristeva, 1980). having been cast out, the abject becomes an ideal container for all the reviled forms of difference by which identity is constituted in language and in culture.

+

so, feral is not nature. not natural. nature has nothing to do with it. and in any case, trust me, nature – poor sap – is over, colonised and doomed. the urban middle-classes got a hold of it, condemned it to that tedious imaginative binary. *nature* was fucked from the day they started bigging it up as a scene of utopian escape, an autonomously functioning idyll, something separate from themselves. they do not perceive the tangled causal relationships between the urban and the wild, or the complex dynamics of hierarchy, erasure, and suppression in which they themselves are hopelessly ensnared. culture fuels this wilful ignorance, promoting nature as an infinitely accessible leisure space, as artistic freight or psychic resource. and if nature *is* escape, aligned with the idea of flight from the pressures of city living, it becomes a site of abdication from shared responsibility, an effectively depoliticised zone. nature was done when some nae-brain decided it was morally uplifting; something they could retreat into or tap to enrich their "spiritual" lives. nature helps the urban centre to hold. nature facilitates the smooth running of its own continued destruction. worse, nature is something to master, a limitless freedom that might, with ingenuity, be brought within the compass of control: literally, through the application of strength; intellectually, through the operation of language.

+

it's all about language. when all you have is a hammer, then all you see are nails. i'm a fucking poet, so of *course* it is about language: who is given permission to speak and how is that speech characterised? what forms of speech are denied the status of "true" language? whose language is figured as cant or cacophony? we will ask with Gayatri Chakravorty Spivak if speech for the *fer*altern subject is ever safe or possible in a language that enables only its limited and colonised forms (Spivak, 1988). how do we describe the destruction or suppression of a language when that same destruction forecloses our ability to articulate this loss; when the hegemonic language we are forced to communicate in is implicated *in* this loss? when we are reduced to gesture, or to manic oscillation between the stutter and the scream? it is *all* about language: between din and "dumbness", spectacle and silence, macabre exhibition and mortified removal.

THE FERAL WHO ARE ALWAYS WITH ME

feral. as a child i heard this word a lot, as applied to children like myself, and to myself, and feral has followed me all the days of my life, and my dwelling has been in the house of feral, if feral had a house, which feral does not. is feral not my shadow? is feral my halo? is feral my secret second self?

+

what should i tell you? that feral will not enrich you. that feral will not be mastered. feral is "wild" without utility. it offers nothing, and it asks for nothing in return. neither instrumental, nor ornamental. you are irrelevant to feral. it repels even your blue, consuming stare, rejects the status of object or tool. feral is surplus, *use*less, gratuitous to the ends of automation; it will be compelled to offer itself for ever more abject labour because its body awkwardly adapted to your demands its skills are not needed, and full employment is *literally* impossible. the feral manifest an excess of everything: time, selves, libidinal energy. there are too many of us, and as individuals we are too loud, too big, an obtruding and tactile reminder of both difference and the inequality that results from difference. feral is the swarm embodied. the horde, the pack, the mob amok. feral is a pest. feral is a weed. feral eats through your mock-tudor timbers, will quake your foundations with its supple, strengthy roots. feral is fear of the site, the estate, the "hood", the ghetto, the slum, the street, the edge. it is fear of the riot. it is fear of the crowd. it is fear of those raw places where feral territories impinge upon tame. it is fear of contagion and invasion. it is fear that the slum itself will spread, and fear that these *others* will overrun their slums. like the living dead, we are coming for you. we outnumber you,

13

lumbering through your palisades, breaching your gated enclaves with a mumbling and shambolic persistence. we can feel ourselves rotting. we like it.

+

the feraltern queer is doubly useless. an avatar of perverse persistence, god's little joke, or a joke against god, a hyena: that patron saint of non-normative reproduction. to an extent all identity is performative, but queer identity is performative in highly specific ways. it resists, to paraphrase Peggy Phelan, the balanced logics of finance: 'it does not save; it only spends'. the feraltern queer recycles itself, cannot be *healed*, only *transformed*, made new. we improvise and reinvent, until we are – once more – all spectacle and no self. smaller and more fabulous with every iteration. cannot stop, only accelerate. *bijou* means jewel. the damage inflicted upon us, we alchemise into fresh resources. we are a kind of circular miracle; queer is generative but *not* reproductive, it manifests excess without the organising principal of lineage or heredity. if the body is the clock and the calendar, then queer-time is an impossible feral futurity, always emerging, forever deferred. to 'spend' and spin towards no recognisable end, but the pursuit of strange affinities, and new, as yet unimagined forms of social relation.

+

or, as Georges Bataille writes, in 'the notion of expenditure' (1985): 'the term poetry, applied to the least degraded and least intellectualised forms of the expression of a state of loss, can be considered synonymous with expenditure; it in fact signifies, in the most precise way, creation by means of loss. its meaning is therefore closer to that of sacrifice.' feral is the candle that consumes itself. it is a poetics of risk, a poetry that risks. at risk. it is an art of discomfort and vulnerability. feral affect is

14

abandonment to a sadness and rage long repressed. it is the endless accumulation of that rage converted into furious delivery: compressed, snarling, flailing, contorted. it is the release of unappeased terror in manic intensity. it is the body, the self, as its sole resource. it is irrational, exhaustive, and exhausting. Joyelle McSweeney tells us that her writing may amount to 'a maximal, dandified, camp, ill-gendered, millenarian text' whose sentences 'run on past health to Death, a region in which the most blasphemous rituals take place' and which demand 'an undue attention to style, flair, garments, gestures rather than actions and plot, descriptions only of things that never were, an uncanny transporting voice not tied to any body, around which flesh accrues and decomposes, a text that does not choose life but might acquire it alongside death' (2015).

+

sit with this thought. what it means to write *alongside death*. i think about this a lot, my own body experiencing various kinds of endometrial pain. i think about the magnified temporality of a body in pain. about pain's relation to labour, the body's relation to value. i can find a way through pain to articulation, but never toward the articulation of pain itself. writing *about* pain makes material the impossible, monotonous nature of writing at all, its masochist's libidiny, its bitter, insatiable spend toward – toward what? the end of the poem is not the end of the pain. nor the end of the self that writes the poem. until, of course, it is. something not merely *impossible*, then, but *futile* to boot. *why are you writing this?* asked nobody, ever. to exhaust this obligated form even as i submit to its physical discomforts and temporal demands. because endometrial pain will not kill me, but because, equally, i cannot be healed. *hysteria* without *climax*. urgent, but without purpose. if writing moves me neither further from my pain nor closer

15

to my death, then where and when is this writing but inside of pain, inside of death? today i am thinking of *persistence*, which is not the same as *resilience* – a word so thoroughly co-opted by the state as to have lost all meaning – but more akin to what Blanchot calls *the passage*, that is 'the exceptional moment when possibility becomes power, when the mind becomes the certainty of a realized form, becomes this body which is form and this beautiful form which is a lovely body. the work is mind, and the mind is the passage' (1955). that is, to collapse this body with that lovely – luminous – body of indefinite, 'never real', ever-open text. obvs. to *persist* is to convert the masochism of endurance into the most sublime – the most supreme – decadence imaginable. to find, after all, that i am (self) indulgent, dreamy, and maximalist against the dictums, temporalities, and logics of literary production, its systems of reduction and demand. the work born of pain will both exceed and withdraw from any pre-determined limit. surpass the circumscribed narrative thrust of suffering, decline, restitution or decease. it is not *functional.* it fails. upwardly.

+

this feral is a site and a mode of failure. i'm not talking about the cute teachable moments of neoliberal fuck-up. you know, how tech bros treat failure as an opportunity to learn, as a milestone to greater, ever-more-tedious success? no, i'm talking about a failure that doesn't fit the dominant culture's masturbatory fantasy of the body as a neutral and broadly behaving instrument. feral encompasses forms, functions, and glitches ordinarily barred from the canon of classical aesthetics. feral will *not* reconstitute its wayward bodies as productive workers, model citizens, or ideal consumer subjects. it will not *heal.* it does not want to get better. feral is the suppressed, clandestine-grotesque body breaking out, ever-open and erupting. feral is multiple and polyvalent, it challenges 'the individual, strictly limited mass, the impenetrable façade' of the normative body so that it summons a commons, a collective, an *us* (Bakhtin, 1984). feral makes other others present in the present, is rampantly relational, an affective solidarity. feral is a failure, is the rejection of the statically perfected individual self as our highest cultural aspiration, will not serve the ends of identity politics, wants a hyenic grammar of irrational possibility. that is, wants to articulate a radical salvation that escapes the toxic logics of competition and success.

+

in the bestiary i meet my own monstrous and failing body. that with which i was born and that which has been interpolated onto me through poverty, through ethnicity and cultural heritage, by sexuality and gender. composite beasts become spurs for thinking about excess, disability, and the ableist, normative recuperation of strange or suffering bodies. but they also point to barely imagined political possibilities. i orbit obsessively the idea of 'a body of dissimilar bodies' as referenced in the opening salvo from the 'symbionese liberation army ('SLA') 'declaration of revolutionary war & the symbionese program' (1974), whose symbol was the seven-headed hydra-like cobra:

the name 'symbionese' is taken from the word symbiosis and we define its meaning as a body of dissimilar bodies and organisms living in deep and loving harmony and partnership in the best interest of all within the body.

in the context of a violent vanguard movement like the SLA this refers to the bringing together of various left-wing struggles – feminist, anti-racist, anti-fascist, etc.– but also to the spontaneous and autonomous functioning of individuals and small groups, working separately, disparately, by various militant methodologies

17

towards the same radical and collective ends. yet 'dissimilar bodies' are also literal bodies, the bodies of those involved in the struggle: racialised bodies, gendered bodies, classed bodies, queer bodies, imprisoned bodies, bodies marked by the military industrial complex, bodies classified as killable waste. while the biological figure for political movements is an old and often unhappy one, in the SLA manifesto it is performing highly specific work: summoning those bodies abjected by difference, and foregrounding the obtruding presence of those the state, in its majesty, prefers not to acknowledge, regards merely as surplus or collateral. the idea of hybrid bodies, especially within the context of black struggle, also gestures to white hysteria surrounding miscegenation, as well as to the fear of queer contagion.

+

what (feral) feminism wants is a miraculous expansion to ways of being in the body, of occupying and extending space, of inhabiting ourselves. again, we came to repopulate the body with new and wondrous modes of being in the body.

+

'body of dissimilar bodies' brings me back to the animal, and to Donna Haraway, writing in *when species meet* of our 'becoming with'. here Haraway argues that living organisms are connected, bound together in what she calls 'material-semiotic nodes or knots in which diverse bodies and meanings co-shape one another'. there is a connection that is prior to the individual organism because every individual organism is constituted in and through 'intra-and interaction'. in other words, all organisms are constituted in relation to many others, blurring the lines between an individual and a community of diverse organisms. this thought has implications, positing an 'intra-action' or an 'encounter' between human and non-human organisms from which we might learn 'an ethics and politics committed to the flourishing of significant otherness' beyond the rules of 'function and calculation' that is 'something not ruled by the logic of the reproduction of the same'.

+

this *flourishing* is feral's utopian aspect. and it bears upon what monsters and so-called monstrous forms can do: how their distortions signal to plenitude, to an excess of meaning that cannot be captured by the tired mimetic representation of everything the world calls "natural". to encounter the body, truly, as a singular, unbearable, irreparable, unrepeatable event. the body as the 'miracle' that illuminates 'transcendence' (Smith, 2018). to enter a state of shock that troubles your knowing calm, your complacency, your smug assurance. a shock that points to an insufficiency of theory, that shakes canons and the value systems that produce them. to receive the de-forming force of our deformity. as if there were no "ugliness". only a hysterical excess of beauty.

+

feral's is a furious utopia. it is a utopia minus hope. hope minus hope. like Gramsci, riffing on Romain Rolland: 'pessimism of the intellect, optimism of the will.' not merely a clear-eyed understanding of how bad things are, but an acknowledgement that the conditions for revolutionary change do not yet exist, see? such change, for Gramsci, could only be brought about through organised, disciplined action. specifically, through the vanguard party seeking to establish a workers' state. what i'm trying to say is that the dictum is not some kind of leftist *live, laugh, love.* the text art of toxic positivity. Gramsci's "hope" – like feral "solidarity" – is a verb and not a noun. it exists only in its active expression. because hope is that other thing co-opted by neoliberal forces as a means of discouraging meaningful action. if hope is neutered from its intended action-oriented nature, then it becomes individualistic and passive, an adult form of wishful thinking, an on-going distraction from the work we are called to do. it's tactical, right? part of a pincer manoeuvre that attempts to deny us the experience of hope through the twin levers of destruction and appropriation. in the first instance, we are robbed of our capacity to hope, to imagine a future with us in it. hope is destroyed by an all-pervasive inequality of access, opportunity and provision; our oppressions are daily, multiple, and utterly exhausting, so much so that they seem absolute and inescapable. we are so consumed with the work of daily survival that our strength is too sapped for anything else. in the second instance, our hope is diverted into self-transcending narratives of ultimate "success". hope is repurposed as idle escape fantasy, or the cut-throat hustle to rise above our class. such narratives are as popular as they are insidious: they paint achieving change – especially economic change, and especially as it concentrates within individual lives – as the sole motivator for working *towards* change. no value is placed on common struggle, no credence is given to the generational and on-going nature of hope. rather, hope becomes a closed circuit: a privatised end, not an open and collective means. fuck that. as China Miéville writes in *the limits of utopia* (2015), for hope to be 'real, and barbed, and tempered into a weapon, we cannot just default to it. we have to test it, subject it to the strain of appropriate near-despair. […] we need utopia, but to try to think utopia, in this world, without rage, without fury, is an indulgence we can't afford. in the face of what is done, we cannot think utopia without hate'. so feral flourishing, a kind of agitating energy, an impossible dream against the doomed limits of the real.

i'm often told my poetry is "depressing". or "angry". i'm described – at best – as some kind of peerless rage machine. and i want to say hey, all of this thrashing around is my trying to temper utopia up in here. they talk about "compassion" and "sympathy" as if these were infinitely renewable resources. they're not. they are painfully finite. the burden of their giving is not shouldered equally by all. maybe my sympathy cannot and will not stretch to meet the irrational demands of my oppressors and class-enemies to be loved. this monstrous and exorbitant fury is feral fighting its way into language, here to make a home. there will be blood.

+

or, call feral a form of negative capability. feral opens and operates within a space of profound discomfort and doubt. this doubt is existential – what am i? what is my meaning, place, and purpose in this world? – and ontological – am i sure that the world itself has meaning? and doubt can duck and dive, past cynical acceptance and saccharine naivety, the prescriptive pressures of instagram optimism, and the despairing resignation to the 'menu' or the 'gift shop' (Halberstam). feral doubt is a holding open against the abbreviating bludgeon of empathy – my solidarity with you is limited by my capacity to imagine *being* you – and the extrovert displays of stifled moral correctness daily demanded of us inside of neoliberal culture – empathy's bloodless and gestural iterations: care emoji, rainbow filter, *u ok, hon?*

+

we need this. for all the times our damaged or disobedient bodies are exceptionalised. for the ways in which able-bodied and mentally healthful dullards condescend to find us inspiring. for the times we are told that suffering is art's nurse, an endlessly ennobling muse. for all the times "cute" disabled children are converted into inspiration-porn by normative bawbegs. for all the times committed communist Frida Kahlo's face appears on a souvenir mug, on a scented candle, on a pair of leggings. for every time a complex and ambivalent experience of bodily habitation is reduced to an emblem of *can-do!* attitude, and raised as an impossible standard against which other suffering bodies will measured.

+

feral is not amenable to cheesy memes. feral is not a *brand*. feral doesn't give a fuck about your brand, about the unconscious, internal panopticon that means we are no longer the *subjects* of coercive state and media control, but the willing apparatus through which this control perpetuates itself, policing and projecting. feral doesn't give a fuck about *influence* or *status*, it isn't on twitter or instagram or tik-tok. feral isn't taking photos of its lunch, or razoring its every waking though into gnomic soliloquies on social media. feral will not participate in your phoney-baloney culture war, the peak liberal dog-shit of cynical "allyship", its dweeby rinsed-out pink-washed pose. feral is interested only in how bodies escape their prescribed categories, and in the moments where those binaries – man, woman, human, non-human – themselves become incoherent and unstable. feral will strike *no* poses, uphold *no* positions. it is not a "demographic". it does *not* have "followers" or court clout. feral cannot be marketed or marketed *at*. it is indigestible to capitalism.

+

hey. 'no single item is dirty apart from a particular system of classification in which it does not fit.' dirt is not an objective attribute of something, merely a 'residual category' of that which is rejected from our 'normal scheme of classifications'. dirt is the name for 'all events which blur, smudge, contradict or otherwise confuse accepted classifications' (Douglas). the feral is *dirty*, is dirt. as doubtful as doubting. feral's incommensurable bodies work to expose the limits of representation; to summon a diversity that exceeds the straight-jacketing of any definite category imposed upon them. in the space that feral opens up we entertain the other, we imagine an other*wise*. feral is outside – at least on the edges – of legibility. you cannot get a handle on feral. you cannot handle feral. feral is, by definition, that which cannot be interpreted or assimilated. although neoliberal culture, in its perpetual cool-hunt, does try: 'when the popular apprehends the subaltern, there is always an act of translation, a re-codification of the subaltern subject and her acts in accordance with the desires of specific populations or publics' (Bishnupriya Ghosh, 2005). that is, if these fuckers can't trap feral behind the bars of the exhibition, they'll tie her to the imitation. they do the other back at the other until the only way the other can perform herself, the only avenue of self-expression left, is through an iteration of those limited, inaccurate tropes: black film actors forced into a continual re-inscription of black suffering and trauma through the roles available to them in mainstream (white) cinema, which naturalises the idea of the black body as inherently persecuted and suffering. white working-class writers expected to enact an identity – jauntily criminal, pathetically victimised, functionally literate – dreamt up by some arse with a Mike Leigh boxset. representational triumph! yay! feral says *fuck that noise*, resists any cohesive and totalising claims to identity, arms herself well against absolute othering. feral invokes 'opacity', calling into question the implied ethical imperatives seeded within the claims of identity politics to visibility – existing within the gaze, within the stare – as an exemplary political platform (Glissant, 1997). it doesn't work. while acknowledgment and inclusion within the broader public sphere has traditionally been the method by which we articulate for recognition and agitate for rights, it has also contributed to our further enmeshment in the apparatus, language, and imagination of the state, and to our public perception as outsiders, interlopers, others. don't believe me? just look at the experience of irish travellers following the recognition of their ethnic status, both in the UK in 2000 and Ireland in 2017. administered. criminalised. recognition handed the state the tools to legislate against traveller communities more effectively. it's a catch. it's a curse. and so? and so instead – tenderly feral – we are embraced in all of our vulnerable fuckèdness, in the granular particularity of our pain and joy. they will grant you visibility to deny you a voice (Judith Butler, 1993). they will define you to corral you, to police and polarise, divide and conquer. but you know better. we all rise, or none of us do.

+

what does it mean to embrace feral, to be embraced by feral? – doggy pong, hot breath, rough tongue – are you afraid? face to face with the wealth of her negative affects – the disappointments, the rage, the isolation, and anxiety – do you run a mile? or do you see the opportunity to puncture the malign functionality, the manufactured consent of contemporary life? for example: heterosex as the trite condition of limit that produces womanhood. to fail this framework is to be unwoman, animal, thing. feral is the thing*ness* that haunts both her acceptable form, and the acceptable forms of her feminism, organised around accommodation and concession as opposed to rejection, mutation, and militant refusal. put it another way: the yoking of animality and womanhood transmitted through art and culture via the ideologically charged woman-as-animal metaphor (cow, bitch, pig, chick, bunny, shrew, etc). the feminised animal is already 'an

24

abject creature, upon whom are ascribed aspects of otherness'
(Donovan, 2016). the feral female is inferior merely for *being*
woman, yet figured as doubly so for not living up to the woman
she's supposed to be. failure squared. all those shitty signifiers
of race and class – accent, grammar, our prole physicality – are
intimately linked to perceptions of femininity, sexual availability,
and moral worth. to be queer, classed, racialised, aged, or disabled
is to be evicted from the hallowed precincts of the feminine, to
join the legions of the feral. don't cry. instead: how dykes undo
gender. queer as anti-theatre, queer as fuck-your-pinkwashed-
feel-good-picnic-my-people-are-dying. you cannot be assimilated
into the airbrushed and agreeable rainbow capitalist borg. you
denounce and incite. you are a saboteur, a walking provocation,
you stick in the throat of neoliberal culture. feral must manifest
what Claude Cahun called 'the courage to be repulsive'. don't
"live your truth". there's no such thing. their "beauty" is a singular
lapse of moral and political nerve.

+

these thoughts drive me back to the bestiary. feral as an allegory
for herself. falls between the literal and the figurative. falls,
entangled in herself. what is this book of beasts in which she is
trapped? the *physiologus*, the grandaddy of all medieval bestiaries,
is a moralising riff on Aristotle's more matter-of-fact – yet still
wildly off-beam – *natural history*. both sets of text were oriented
towards the accumulation of knowledge about the natural world,
but Aristotle's medieval imitators seemed driven by the need
to situate that knowledge within the compass of a christian
metaphysics. feral says they were afraid of the Fall. one of Adam's
original perfections was an encyclopaedic knowledge of nature.
this knowledge was lost at the Fall, and bestiary texts often feel
like a sweaty attempt to recuperate that kind of unattainable

mastery (Harrison, 2006). the animal becomes fixed in language and in form. our nature is knowable through – and equivalent to – the commentary that accretes around it. feral falls through. the meanings swoon in reason. if god spoke, and, as in paradise lost, 'the earth obey'd and straight/ op'ning her fertile womb teem'd at a birth/ innumerous living creatures, perfect forms' (Milton, 1667), then what should the good encyclopaedist make of or do with those multiple *im*perfect forms? corralled within yet excluded from prevailing conceptions of *nature*. for example, the 'yena', 'hyaena', 'gulo', 'leucrota', 'crocuta', 'corocotta', leucrocuta', 'akabo', 'alzabo', 'zabo', 'ana', 'belbus', 'lupus vesperitinus', 'zilis', 'lacata', 'hyen', etc. the hyena flickers across the bestiary, a savvy escapist, a quick-change artist, a deceitful, shape-shifting mutant. the profusion of her appearances speaks to an obsessive anxiety, not only about the protean nature of the hyenic body, but about naming itself, and our need to locate particular kinds of human domination within and through language. if the need to nail the hyena to the page is, in part, a contest of mastery, then perhaps her very multiplicity is an expression of doubt as to the ultimate victor in that contest. etymologies are crucial components of bestiary texts, but prone as they are to elaborate invention and bizarre distortion, they form ever-more baroque and desperate attempts at capture and containment. attempts the hyena skilfully evades (de Hamel, 2008).

+

hyenas are like weeds. like bad ideas. you cut them down and they spring back up, twice as virulent and feisty as before. poltergeists. vermin. never quite exorcised from territory or consciousness. they are a haunting, an incursion. sir Walter Raleigh, in his *history of the world* (1614), claims of the hyena that it was excluded from Noah's ark. according to Raleigh, only 'pure' species were saved, not mongrels or hybrids. stranger still, hyenas somehow reproduced themselves after the deluge, through the unseemly union between a dog and a cat (White, 1984). hyena a swaggering survivalist, pivoting between and strutting across categories of species and sex, so that 'we might marvel at how the hyena changes function, and a moment ago a female, taken from behind by a male, is now a male' (Ovid). hyena as Valerie Solanas, erupting with queer and prescient rage to tell us we no longer need men, that 'retaining the male has not even the dubious purpose of reproduction' (Valerie Solanas, 1967). the likely source for the myth of the hyena's sex-shifting ability is the female spotted hyena's genitalia. her clitoris extends an astonishing eight inches, and is shaped and positioned exactly like a penis. they can even get erections. further, the spotted hyena's labia have fused to form a false scrotum, swollen with fatty tissue. as if that were not sufficient, the female spotted hyena is unique among mammals in that she has no external vaginal opening, instead she must urinate, copulate, and give birth through her multi-purpose "pseudo-penis". this last often entails fatal consequences for the hyena, with ten percent of first-time mothers dying in childbirth; for her cubs things are no less precarious: the hyena's birth canal is twice the length of similar-sized mammals, with a sharp turn halfway down. up to sixty percent of cubs suffocate during birth as a result. female spotted hyenas are "unnatural" and ill-adapted mothers; they are bigger and more aggressive than their male counterparts, whom they dominate sexually. the sight of a large, aggressive "male" animal, giving birth through its "penis" is undoubtedly the foundation for the myth of the hyena's hermaphroditic flex. but. even now, long after the originating misconception has been corrected, unease persists. it isn't merely that hyenas flip our relentlessly naturalised gender norms; their bodies actively sabotage the biological processes out of which and through which gender categories are constituted and maintained. i've read more than one paper, asking, with varying degrees of levity, what can possibly be the "point" or the "purpose" of an animal "designed" to die in childbirth? whose body is so actively hostile to the life it incubates? the subtext is that hyenas are aberrations, both surplus and counter to the ends of evolution. hyena becomes a queer clarion because she demands a painful expansion of the canon of the natural, or else because she destroys it outright. for all of us with bodies that betray and fail the reproductive imperatives demanded of them, the hyena can be an icon. while writing *hyena! jackal! dog!* (2021) my obsessive hyenic research led me back to ireland. specifically to the area around cork, 45,000 years ago. there were hyenas in ireland 45,000 years ago. in the national museum of ireland in dublin, i stared at a prehistoric hyena jawbone, and at the grey, granular thunderstone of its faeces. it is indicative of my mental state at the time that i found these commonplace traces strangely moving. moving *because* they were commonplace. they represented the limitless horizon of a land not yet named or freighted, and of a creature not yet subject to scrutiny and classification.

+

the hyena is a scavenger. that is, a synanthropic survivalist. something of this tenacity is captured in Raleigh's assertion that they were excluded from the ark. their uncanny queer endurance. a synanthropic species troubles the boundaries between human and non-human, repurposing 'anthropogenic resources' towards their own ends, and existing – even thriving – in environmental – perhaps political – edgelands typically hostile to life (Seegert, 2014). synanthropes are border-steppers, and the hyena is a border-stepper par excellence. ireland is a border country, that is both a country fraught with borders – geographic, political, linguistic, religious, cultural – and itself a kind of border or limit. a place the english imagination halts or baulks at, the end of god's speed and good civility. perhaps that is why the idea of hyenas in ireland holds such fascination and appeal to me. or perhaps it is the long legacy of representation that burdens irish persons with animalistic – specifically wolfish and hyenic – traits.

+

in medieval bestiary texts, 'nonbinary sex could be mobilised as a vicious tool to denigrate non-christian and racially "othered" subjects' (DeVun, 2021). non-normative bodies were themselves objects of anxiety and repulsion, but they also functioned as expedient metaphors for presenting racialised others – africans, muslims, jews, the irish – as a subhuman threat, to be exiled to the cartographic limit of christianity, or whose polluting presence was the proper subject of sanitary intervention and colonial control. for example, the *physiologus* compares the hyena's sexual ambiguity to the 'ambiguity of faith' exhibited by 'the jews, who were first faithful and afterwards idolatrous', as well as to bad faith christians, seduced to sensuality and greed (Baxter, 1998). or consider the dog-heads, the cynocephali, how, in christian iconography, Saint Christopher was so often depicted as belonging to this cannibal transhuman tribe. of course. a savage race of dog-like aspect, physically transfigured through baptism, is a potent allegory – and argument – for the redemptive power of faith, crusade, and conversion. similarly, and earlier still, the *topographia hiberniae* (1188) depicts the irish as bestial beings who express their inhumanity through intercourse with animals. werewolves are a significant feature of this text: sometimes virtuous, but more often appearing as a race of treacherous, human-shaped irishmen, exemplars of low-cunning, and dirty animality. this characterisation has persisted. John Taylor would come to metaphorise the killing of protestants by howling 'irish wolves', and Heylyn described an irish race as behaving 'scarcely like men'. for Cromwell the irish were simply 'beasts' (Bartlett, 2010), candidates all for occupation, imprisonment, exile or extermination.

+

wolves were one of the first known targets of animal destruction, and they became extinct in ireland by 1770, an active project of annihilation that ran concurrently with Cromwell's determined – but by no means novel – efforts to exterminate the irish language. attempts to render ireland less 'savage' through the suppression and control of its language had been frequent throughout the sixteenth and seventeenth centuries. the 1537 Act for the English Order, Habit and Language stated that in ireland 'the english tongue' must be 'used by all men', associating 'diversity' of language with a 'savage and wild kind and manner of living' among irish persons. a 1657 proclamation stated that citizens must raise their children to speak only english or face forcible transplantation to connaught (a territory then reserved for those who continued to practice catholicism despite laws to the contrary). Edmund Spenser's hysterical polemic *a view of the present state of ireland* (1596) claimed that the irish were in the habit of eating wolves, forming various relationships with them, and ultimately transforming into them. the text presents the irish as 'creeping forth' on all fours from every corner of the 'woods and glynnes' to 'eate the dead carrions', not as a consequence of the famine which the english 'planters' had themselves engineered, but as a result of their animalistic nature. this intimate association of the irish with wild animal behaviour of the most abject kind has a poetic, but also a deeply political basis, justifying an english (and protestant) ascendancy achieved through brutality and neglect. Spenser diagnosed the barbarism of irish culture in order to demonstrate a need for 'the reducing of that savage nation to better government and civilitye'. he infamously advocated for induced famine as a tool to create the necessary conditions for a viable english settlement in ireland. he was not the only one to deploy such logics. as early as 1610, Lord Blennerhasset, chief baron of the irish exchequer, describes outlaw 'woodkernes' who reside in the forest as 'human wolves' who ought to be tracked down 'to their lairs' and destroyed (Neeson, 1997). At one stroke, deforestation becomes a potent symbolic act; political resistance is repeatedly coded as inherently bestial, with the hunting of both wolves and dissenting humans celebrated and rewarded by the state. ireland's status as a colony has long been linked to its identity as a fearful and fascinating 'wolf-land' for the occupying english. this feral disobedience concentrates in irish tongues and irish bodies. in the 1650s a captain in General Ireton's regiment described the slaughter of an irish garrison at cashel: he claimed that among the bodies were found 'divers that had tails near a quarter of a yard long' (Thomas, 1983). the amorphous hybrid nature of those bodies justifies the logic of producing them. feral subjects. irishness as uncanny queer.

+

feral fails the identities ascribed to her, outstrips the expectations lodged in the eye of the beholder. is not beholden, seldom held. teeth and a tail. who do they mean when they say *girl, white girl?* and by white the sleekness and symmetry from which an ideal white identity is constituted, and in which shape white aesthetic, moral, and political judgements are cast. what does it mean to "fail" at white the way that irish and traveller people have always failed? Charles Kingsley, writing from ireland in 1860, describes irish people as not merely racially inferior, but subhuman, an assessment that exists in profound tension with their white skin: 'i am haunted by the human chimpanzees i saw along that hundred miles of horrible country. […] [t]o see white chimpanzees is dreadful; if they were black one would not see it so much, but their skins, except where tanned by exposure, are as white as ours.' *as ours.* to recruit and address by implication an ideal white audience who share a consensus identity, language and culture. his is not merely an appeal to this invisible cohort, rather their very existence lends his argument force and legitimacy, irresistibly dividing the world into *us* – rational, cultivated, enlightened – and *them* – abhorrent, primitive, dirty and stupid. Kingsley goes on to echo this motif of the simian irish in the water-babies (1863), especially in the passage where he describes why the blessed Saint Brendan had no luck in converting the 'wild irish', a race who would not heed his christian message, preferring instead 'to brew potheen, and dance the pater o'pee, and knock each other over the head with shillelaghs, and shoot each other from behind turf dykes, and steal each other's cattle, and burn each other's homes [...] [t]he people who would not hear him were changed into gorillas, and gorillas they are until this day.' Kingsley's was not a minority perception, such animal comparisons were a mainstay of victorian anti-irish racism, popularised during the famine through political cartoons such as 'the british lion and the irish monkey' which appeared in *Punch* in 1848. 'the irish monkey' is an image capable of transmitting both pity and vicious contempt; deployed to provoke hedged sympathy and open ridicule. the caricature of an animalised irish populace functions as a rationalisation for colonial control, so much so that the poverty in which irish persons existed came to be understood as part of the national character, not something that was *done* to people, but a product of their culture and their race; poverty itself racialised the irish and produced a particular kind of hatred: while black and brown others were abjected and oppressed for and through their essential difference, these white others could only ever be degraded, impure versions of a pristine white ideal. a mockery, a betrayal, a throwback. or (worse) not a lower order of human life, but simply not human at all.

+

as irish in england we were still white n***ers and bog-w*gs throughout the eighties and nineties. these school-yard pejoratives expose the way poverty operates to remove us from the precincts of whiteness. white n***er is effective as a slur because it communicates not merely revulsion, but that very specific sense of betrayal; it cancels, even as it calls into being, an impossible body, an unthinkable presence, a walking contradiction. white n***er manifests the shock felt by Charles Kingsley passing exhausted and destitute irish bodies on the road. his stare converts an occasion for sympathy into abject spectacle by refusing the humanity of those his eye encounters. it is necessary for Kingsley to dehumanise the irish. as it has been necessary for many others, before and since, both to manage the cognitive dissonance provoked by christian pretensions (on the one hand), and barbaric treatment of the other (on the other). but also to justify, through the mechanism of cultural representation, the apathy with which that suffering other is met.

+

end up in a row trying to explain to an angry nineteen-year-old that yes, racism against white others exists, but it can only exist through the prior and absolute denigration of the black body. think about Edmund Spenser and *the faerie queene* (1596), the effortful white epistemology of that book, where irish bodies and ecologies are considered foul, twisted, corrupt, and corrupting according to their distance from – and eternal antagonism towards – white (english, protestant) transcendental norms. when Spenser wants a to conjure an image of seething falsehood or monstrous fecundity, he reaches for africa. take Errour and Duessa. the way Spenser aligns Errour's blackness with african blackness through simile, africa already being metonymic for various types of repulsive otherness within the english imagination. and Duessa, her name itself containing a corruption of the irish word for "black". black belongs to all those who must be marked. for this process to work, you first have to decide that visible forms of blackness are abhorrent and disgusting. Errour's children are described as 'deformed monsters, fowle and blacke as inke', and Spenser connects the bogs of ireland to the mud of the nile; both producing monstrous shapes through spontaneous generation.

what i am trying to tell him is that of course they hate us, and of course it hurts. but the originating wound is not in white flesh. we rid ourselves of anti-irish racism not by competing with anti-black racism in a hierarchy of suffering, but in vigilant repair of that originating wound. poor white others struggle with this sometimes, especially young men. when they're told they have privilege they get angry because they are powerless. nobody has ever explained that privilege isn't power. those who hold the latter would like us to forget that.

+

what differentiates the "white n***er" from her black or brown sister is the ambiguous boon of "passing": the assumption of a single, shared white identity ("*ours*") that can be courted and played to in a way that is impossible for the visibly other. to enter into both the privilege and shame of "passing" is, in some sense, to accept and internalise the judgments that necessitated your doing so, about yourself and about other others. it is to feel like a fraud even in the white skin that envelops you. if this is true anywhere, it is certainly true within elite literary and cultural spaces. what's the phrase for it? *dog in a manger*: to occupy a place or a position you are unequal to, unworthy of. Your presence in these spaces can be nothing but an unwelcome hindrance to others better suited than yourself. This feeling is often called "imposter syndrome", but I don't like that phrase: it concentrates the problem in some inner subjective realm peculiar to those who experience it, when in reality those same subjects are merely reacting to the ambient social conditions that shape their world. you have *not* been welcome or encouraged. you are *not* the implied audience for art and culture. if you find yourself here, you have no right to be where you are, you have arrived by sinister or duplicitous means. to typify the vague constellation of tropes assembled around you is to be inferior in every way. but to be seen as *a*typical is to add transgression and trespass to your long list of sins. feral returns as the unruly child of a trickster god: as "gentry", a changeling baby who looks just like you. "passing" is deceit and the fear of being found out. it is to live within a series of endlessly competing performances in which class, ethnicity, and sexuality mirror and undercut one another across cycles of concealment and disclosure. you cannot fulfil the expectations of otherness, but neither can you conform to the strictures and limits of your "own" community and culture. feral *always* exceeds, will not stay in its lane, can find no perfect expression of solidarity, and no true home in any one territory or lexical field. feral does not know *how* to belong, is forever searching for a way to make the unhomely home make room for her, to exist in a world that rejects her, to love what does not love her back. the source of her howl is a yearning to establish this home, a place of peace and safety. her howl is the desperate extension of affection towards a commons of nameless others. it is a love without impetus or object. it is looking for somewhere to land.

+

when i was born my mother's dog ate a portion of my umbilical cord. this story has assumed the status of both a family legend, and an explanation for my lifelong preference for canids over people: i have belonged to the dog ever since. but it also elicits squeamish incredulity, conjures for others a scene of near-dystopian squalor and neglect, a home in which the hygienic boundary between human and non-human members had become hopelessly porous. *how would the dog get a hold of your cord?* eyebrows raised. the story provokes a profound anxiety; hints at a close, unwholesome contact with the animals we kept. insanitary, yes, but also somehow morally disturbing. this specific kind of unease seemed to originate – or was especially virulent – within nineteenth century discourses of poverty, animality, and disease. in victorian london, middle-class social concern with the "slum" gave rise to a wealth of investigative literature attempting to account for, explore, and contain the growing spectre of urban poverty. this work was apt to focus on the "inhuman" conditions in which the poor eked out their existence, often in fraught, claustrophobic association with their animals. the basis for this relationship was economic and practical: space was at a premium, and where else could the poor be expected to house the living instruments of their livelihood? animal bodies were also valuable sources of warmth and protection. yet to middle-class observers such proximity served to develop a physical and spiritual resemblance between the poor and their animals. both were seen to suffer from and contribute to the filth and misery of their environment. this idea is best exemplified in the victorian horror of rabies. in 1896 the times reported that rabies in ireland was "rife"; it went on to speculate that dogs from ireland were responsible for numerous outbreaks in england. (Jeanne Dubino, 2014). in the collective consciousness of victorian england, the threat of rabies from ireland was greater than from almost anywhere else in the world, and this notion was entirely related to the status of irish persons as uncivilised interlopers, barbarians at the gate. rabies itself produced in the human beings affected by it an animal-like transformation reminiscent of Gower's biblical 'curse'. people became troubling hybrids, a mass of inarticulate and compromised humanity, qualities already ascribed to irish immigrant populations in london. stereotypes of the irish, transmitted through political cartoons and "satirical" newspapers, presented them as simian, animalistic, and racially inferior. the panic caused by rabies provided an occasion to express a variety of shared class and racial hatreds; to give vent to the terror of miscegenation, and to further attempt to control or contain the slum in the interests of health and hygiene – both literal and moral.

+

pre-empting the hysteria surrounding rabies, Henry Mayhew, writing in *london labour and the london poor* (1864) describes conditions in cholera-stricken bermondsey in the following visceral way:

> the water is covered with a scum almost like a cobweb, and prismatic with grease. in it float large masses of green rotting weed, and against the posts of the bridges are swollen carcasses of dead animals, almost bursting with the gases of putrefaction. along its shores are heaps of indescribable filth, the phosphoretted smell from which tells you of the rotting fish there, while the oyster shells are like pieces of slate from their coating of mud and filth. in some parts the fluid is almost as red as blood from the colouring matter that pours into it from the reeking leather-dressers' close by.

[...]

at the back of nearly every house that boasts a square foot or two of outlet – and the majority have none at all – are pig-sties. in front waddle ducks, while cocks and hens scratch at the cinderheaps. indeed the creatures that fatten on offal are the only living things that seem to flourish here […]

Mayhew is broadly sympathetic, his aim was to improve social conditions for the poor, to draw attention to their plight and to lift them out of misery, yet even he can't resist an evocation of poor persons as an equally victimised and degenerate collective whose identities threaten to merge with that of their animals. dogs in particular are everywhere in *london labour and the london poor*: they are a means of economic survival, they offer a form of protection, a crude sort of sport. terriers are turned loose on rats, hounds are set to catch rabbits, mastiffs and bulldogs are forced to fight for the entertainment of the crowd. there is a great deal of animal cruelty in Mayhew's book, perpetrated by a poor populace who themselves had been ill-used and brutalised. it's striking how the discourses surrounding poor others use both fear of animality and concern over the welfare of actual animals as opportunities to perform a number of ideas about class and race. for the victorian middle classes in particular, a refinement of feeling towards "dumb beasts" constituted an ideal expression of white middle-class identity; it was evidence of sensitivity, a niceness of feeling that could never be expected of the lumpen-proles. to put it more neatly, condescension towards animals is proof of humanity and civilisation. but only certain animals are deserving of this care, and feral humans are absolutely exempt. further, it is only the personal, viscerally embodied cruelty of the poor that merits disapprobation, and not the sets of industrial processes that designate entire animal populations as expendable, killable.

a paradox emerges: the poor are denigrated for their treatment of dumb animals, and yet it is the animal behaviour of the poor that rationalises their brutalising and neglectful treatment at the hands of their social betters. this does not compute. it short-circuits the foundational logics of the nature/culture divide. it calls into question the legitimacy of that divide itself. it raises questions about what it means to be civilised, what it means to be cultured, what it means to be human.

+

in the interviews that Mayhew conducted, a number of indigent persons would describe being treated no better 'than a dog'; they would eat scraps from the gutter like dogs, they would resemble dogs in their whipped, defeated posture; the same arbitrary abuse would be meted out to them as to dogs. in one particularly haunting passage a man tells Mayhew: 'ah, sir, that's what it is to be a poor man; to have your poverty flung in your teeth every minute. people says, "to be poor and seem poor is the devil"; but to be poor, and be treated like a dog merely because you are poor, surely is ten thousand times worse.' when the victorian middle classes talked about kindness towards animals, they did not mean those dogs. they meant the imagined menageries of Charles Burton Barber, best known for his wildly popular and highly sentimental portraits of dogs. my favourite – if that can possibly be the right word – is 'the reading lesson'. in it, a little girl – immaculately dressed and spotlessly clean – holds an open book under the chin of her faithful and patient bloodhound. her eyes are directed downwards toward the text, but the dog looks up at her with soulful and loving fidelity. my mother jokes that this is a gentrified reimagining of myself as a child, combining as it does my twin passions: dogs and books. but Barber's world is a far cry from our own. it is an oddly textureless world, odourless and orderly. the dog has no genitals. the child is too clean. there is no saliva, no dirt; no fug of breath or sense of repressed movement. Barber's bloodhound is made an equal participant in a spiritually uplifting cultural activity situated in a very proper victorian drawing room. it is both ludicrous and neutered. it confirms a suspicion i have often entertained about the english middle classes, that they are not in fact a "nation of animal lovers". they love their *pets*, where "pet" is something you do to "animal" to make it proper for that drawing room; where "pet" is a kind of prosthesis, the subject of a misty-eyed and reality-adverse attachment. this attachment is only ever a tasteful veil drawn over a craving for status and social position. that's a kind of love that is alien to me. that's the kind of love that allows people to cherish their hounds and tear apart the fox. to coo over lambs in a field, then go home and eat one with potatoes and onion gravy. yeah. victorian britain racialised and gendered animals to a bizarre degree. english dog breeds were considered morally, intellectually, and physiologically superior to the dogs of the "colonies", which were, for the most part, not classified into breeds at all.

+

feral springs from this: from a universe that abjures animal-like humans, but imagines for itself a race of human-like animals: animals without edges. never sick, never difficult. there's a strong survival of that victorian sensibility in england. catch glimpses of it in the twits who airbrush their dogs' genitals out of photographs on facebook. the nice, polite ladies in hunter wellies and quilted gilets who stop you in the park to harangue you about your "status-symbol dog", your "dangerous dog". the same women who bought their pedigree pets from kennel club puppy farms: places that put to death the dogs that do not meet their breed-specific standards. these dogs are inbred, they wheeze when they breathe, their bones are so brittle they spend half their lives in surgery.

yet it is always *your* dog deemed to be equally endangered and dangerous. funny how. historically, representations of ethnic and cultural others have tended to dehumanise their subjects, but depictions of irish and traveller people conflate persons and their animals to an unusually high degree. in the iconography of anti-irish racism, a dog of mean and cunning cast is both an extension of and a figure for the violence and cunning of the humans to which it belongs. the dangerous dog offers a legitimating occasion for racist, classist sentiments. the mastiff or pit bull-type dog does not merely possess a characteristic savagery; it is also material evidence of that quality in the people who care for it. although "care" is the wrong word. we cannot love our dogs, for we ourselves are dog-like and incapable of love. our dogs are intended to engender fear in others, weaponised and threatening. "tactical". these types of discourse use both fear of the dog and an expression of concern for its treatment as a mechanism for indulging centuries old prejudice. an equivalence is drawn between ourselves and our animals: the dog is evoked in its most negative aspect, and we are supposed to share those menacing characteristics; to be unpredictable and savage. framing negative characterisations of irish and traveller people through the lens of animal welfare allows the middle classes to vent both their racism and their classism while simultaneously performing an idealised and virtuous (white, middle-class) humanity.

+

feral isn't fooled. and you cannot truly "love" animals if you are using them as the basis for a dehumanising comparison. pejorative animal comparisons do not merely suggest a psychical resemblance between their human target and the metaphorised animal. rather, a portion of the disgust or fear felt toward the animal is transferred to that person. this is why i feel such an intense kinship with dogs in particular, having been imaginatively bracketed together for so long.

+

as a small child i did my dogginess in literal-minded and extrovert ways: i would go about on all-fours, ask to be given my food and drink from bowls on the floor. i would make dog noises, i would follow our dog into her basket and snuggle against her often grudging flank. if i fought physically with other children (which i did, often) my signature move was to sink my teeth in. hard. this behaviour was "crazy", but i knew i wasn't a dog. i identified *with* not *as* the animals around me, and my dog performance was not delusion but an (over)zealous expression of solidarity. put it another way, the dog's mode of life and manner of expression felt better suited to the things i needed to say, either because i lacked the language for those things, or because the intensity of my emotions exceeded the language i had been given to work with, what it was appropriate or permissible to think, say, do in any given context. to exist inside the animal, to enact the animal, was a way of resisting everything implied by humanness, femaleness. the dog was an exit, a form of refusal. as Aaron M. Moe notes, animals communicate not only with signs, but through their embedded capacity to gesture, taking part in a process of 'bodily poiesis' (2013). as a child, this seemed self-evident: dogs absolutely had a unique way of languaging the world, of exhibiting agency within their environment. i wanted to participate in that language, that agency.

+

i remember i had an LP of Disney's *the jungle book*. i loved the musical numbers, but wanted to hear more from the wolves, and was utterly baffled by Mowgli's decision to re-join the village and the world of men. when i was later given a copy of Kipling's book i was horrified. book-Mowgli conquers and subdues his way through a series of violent animal encounters. not fun at all. both versions of the text centre on the impossibility of equal human-animal relations, but the book – and Mowgli's story in particular – is such an explicit allegory for empire and colonialism that it makes you want to puke. Kipling's racist, unionist dogma would come to ruin my once-beloved record, but as a young child i was simply confused by a story that resolved itself in a such a disappointing way, reassimilating Mowgli into human society with its predetermined paths and predictable routines.

+

dogs were avatars of freedom. growing up, they ran fairly wild, where "wild"' is both a territory and a state of being. escapes and impromptu matings were common; out walking, you would often cross paths with a dog in the road. they were not strays, but they were not beholden to their humans either. they seemed to live alongside, in a world of their own. in their autonomous, parallel existence i seemed to sense, as Donna Haraway writes, that: 'dogs are not about oneself. indeed, that is the beauty of dogs. they are not a projection, nor the realization of an intention, nor the telos of anything. they are dogs'. Haraway goes on to describe them as 'a species in an obligatory, constitutive, historical, protean relationship with human beings. the relationship is not especially nice; it is full of waste, cruelty, indifference, ignorance, and loss, as well as of joy, invention, labor, intelligence, and play' (Haraway, 2003). i did not have the language for this thought, but it was as much in their irreducible difference as in their similarity to my own psychic and social condition that dogs compelled – continue to compel – me. in many ways i too was "wild", and of the wild. on the british mainland, in the west country, this wildness had both its sinister and idyllic aspects. mine was not a cosseted or overly-scrutinised childhood, and i miss the hours unaccounted for, those hours reserved for being and becoming lost. i miss those hours despite everything. the private lives of children are often secretive and hazardous, and the "wild" has its own rules, its own code of silence; it teaches its own harsh lessons, especially to girls. the dogs in their sauntering freedom were vulnerable. we envied them, but they lived in proximity to danger. they *were* danger too. we would follow a loose dog for hours, watching it lope its inscrutable errands. at times the dog would tire of us, turning to give chase, all hackles and teeth. we would scatter, whooping, delighted and scared. not merely of being bitten but, obscurely, of being rejected, shut out of a world we could enter only at the edges to begin with. a dog was a riddle: simultaneously 'ours' and its own. it had that independence, a peculiar self-possession. this is the enduring fascination of the dog, why my earliest drawings were of dogs. why a dog was the lyric subject of my first ever poem. why my favourite stories had canine protagonists. in my games of make-believe, i was either a dog, or else i incorporated the dogs around me, casting them as sidekicks, oracles, and heroes. i was an avid collector of dog memorabilia, and an irritatingly precocious font of canid lore. my earliest and best companions were dogs; they were my lone constant, a reassuring presence in a life spent isolated and on the move.

+

i discovered Jack London's novels, *the call of the wild* and *white fang*, before i could truly comprehend them. the former describes a decent into feral, the other is a journey towards domestication. of the two, i preferred *the call of the wild*, in which Buck, the novel's canine protagonist, must embrace his wild ancestry in order to survive in an unforgiving and alien country. i understood that. but the story's special appeal lay also in the fact that the animals in other books were cast in valorous or sentimental roles; they had noble thoughts and enlightened values. they weren't very animal at all, and for me, the otherness of the animal – the *animalness* of the animal – was the point. i recognised the dog in Buck, and i was captured by London's attempt to "get at" animal consciousness – which exists necessarily without (human) language – through language. London and i came to a parting of the ways on the day i happened across *the people of the abyss* (1903). informed by a similar social concern as Mayhew's much earlier work, *the people of the abyss* is a first-hand account of the several weeks the author spent living in the whitechapel district of the east end in 1902. in it, London attempts to experience what life was like for the poor of whitechapel, and to understand the poor themselves. in this last ambition he is singularly doomed, and *the people of the abyss* becomes just one more work in which the poor are inseparable from the horror that is happening to them; the abyss is not merely an address; it is an innate condition. in one particularly uncomfortable passage, London writes:

> for an hour past, the air has been made hideous by a free-for-all, rough-and-tumble fight going on in the yard that is back to back with my yard. when the first sounds reached me i took it for the barking and snarling of dogs, and some minutes were required to convince me that human beings, and women at that, could produce such a fearful clamour. drunken women fighting! it is not nice to think of; it is far worse to listen to (p.25)

it wasn't just that i knew those sounds or could imagine those women and the exhausted extremity that pushed them to such a pitch. and it's not as if London were wrong. it isn't *nice.* but for Jack London it was also an objectless assault on the senses of their betters; it was primitive and bestial: dog-like. reading this i found it impossible to fathom how somebody could write of animal others – especially dogs – with such insight, and of human others with such a myopic lack of empathy. if London has such an abiding respect for and understanding of dogs, why were dogs the mechanism through which he denied destitute women their humanity? *women.* of course, the missing piece of the puzzle is that London's animals are male. the women brawling in the back doubles were not merely animalistic, but *feral*, where feral is a paradox: yes, it *is* animal, but it is also "unnatural", that is grotesque, dissipated, debauched, unmotherly, unwomanly.

+

the way literature and the law use "unnatural" is complex and contradictory. what, after all, constitutes an "unnatural" action, an "unnatural act"? queer pleasures, certainly, and a motley assortment of other human practices. but what vexes and provokes is how entangled the nature/culture divide is in this thinking, and how quickly it descends into impossible absurdity: on one hand, human beings are the actors, inflicting harm from the outside in. the crime is *against* nature itself. nature is the victim, the injured party. and yet, the humans who commit unnatural acts are said to be behaving *like* animals. which is it? you can't be guilty of damaging nature from without while being reviled for "regressing" to a "natural" state. perhaps the real crime, the real injury, is damage dealt to the nature/culture divide itself, which is not merely ruptured under the force of our feral acts, but its very foundational logics short-circuited. queer women perform this short-circuit, poor women certainly do. and poor, queer women? well.

+

i remember feeling betrayed by London, as i would later feel betrayed by a lot of the men i admired and a number of the books they had written. this feeling of ambient disappointment would follow and assail me at various points throughout my life, that feeling of being forced to occupy the most abject edge of even metaphor. i saw possible versions of my future lived by men and boys, so i would attempt to attach myself to their cohorts, to do as they did, and it took me a long time to understand why i was constantly rebuffed, why time and again i found myself ridiculed, targeted, ejected. my identity as "girl" was supposed to supersede or cancel everything else i tried to be or do. as a "girl" i would profane the thing i loved through corrosive contact with it. women and girls are still being told that we have invaded and "ruined" a formerly male preserve (comics, punk, Marxism), as if male were not merely the originator but also the default. i liked "boy things". my body was an angular mass of fidgets, my hair when it grew was a thicket of honey-blonde knots. i bit my nails, i rolled in the dirt. i climbed trees and frequently fell out of them. i was unequal to the dresses my grandfather brought for me. i loved their important gaudiness; their swags and ruffles and flounces, but i trashed them soon as look. all of my clothes became torn or stained. i didn't want them to. i wanted to wear the dress and climb the tree, but the hem would snag on a branch; i'd lose buttons and bows to a tussle with gravity or dogs. i couldn't have both. someone was always telling me that: *you can't have both.* so i stopped wearing dresses. i cut my hair short. i was a "tomboy", a "toughie", and if i wanted to do the things i wanted to do then i had to be. you *become* feral to live in the world, to survive. but what the world makes of you – even on that very small scale – the world refuses to accept.

+

i wanted to be a boy in the same way as i wanted to be a dog, so far as i envied boys their luminous masculine reach, their way of being in the world, their mercurial possibility, the vividness of even their suffering. men spoke and did. they were spoken about. men wrote books about men speaking and doing. they were the subject of extensive lyric and dramatic treatment. there were questions asked about them in parliament. they had their pictures in the paper. i can't remember hearing a single song about the women prisoners in armagh jail. ever. the blanket protests, dirty protests, and hunger strikes conducted by their male counterparts in long kesh had infiltrated our lives at a cellular level. the family talked. and talked. exemplary male sacrifice was everywhere. the women's no wash protest was never sung and barely spoken of, presumably because male shit was considered less disgusting than menstrual blood. the women in armagh jail were serially degraded and abused: strip-searched and sexually assaulted as a matter of policy, but the language did not exist for the specific pain of *their* treatment; an embarrassed silence hung over them all. i think the catholic church had trained us for this silence. male suffering may be exemplary, honourable, possessed of a refining fire. men endure what is done to them, they transmute abuse into heroism. female pain is only ever squalid, there is no dignity in *our* survival – no grace – just a grubby and stubborn persistence. when we are abused, a portion of the perpetrator's sin adheres to us. the church venerates those murdered virgin saints because survival itself is the medium of our shame, its receptacle and conduit. men may suffer and die for a cause. women have no cause. they suffer because they are women. this vulnerability is sordid. on the mantel: a row of dead women with the arrested pre-pubescent bodies of olympic gymnasts; they smiled benignly as their torturers lopped and gouged at their perfect porcelain limbs.

as a child i often felt confused, understanding on some level that men *en masse* were the enemy, yet identifying myself with specific men and boys – in life and in fiction – because i saw men and boys moving through the world in ways i could imagine or desire for myself; i found reflections of my own rage and frustration in their art and in their politics. i didn't ask myself where is the rage of women? i couldn't see it, and so i assumed it didn't exist. but – a kernel of doubt – if x and i were kindred spirits, how was i to interpret their hatred and cruelty *toward* women and girls? ignore it? internalise it? mentally separate myself from the category of "girl" because i wasn't like that, they didn't mean me? the boys in my life would tell me all the time "you're not like other girls", which functioned as a compliment or an accusation, depending on their mood. i was uneasy: how would they *know* what other girls were like? all of them? really? but on a certain level i was also flattered. to be thought of as different or special is a salve to the child-ego bruised by a daily litany of insults and abuses. i was seduced by that. i wouldn't be the first, suckered into seeing other girls as deficient or unworthy; myself as the exception to a general rule of quivering uselessness. divide and conquer. it's the way they sew everything up: if she won't compete with other women toward the same arbitrary ideal, isolate her in her "unique" rejection of that ideal, puff her up with the way she "sees through" it, how "intelligent" she is, how "wise beyond her years." make her proud, superior and lonely. it doesn't matter how it's done, so long as they're not comparing notes. so long as they're not looking to each other for solidarity or comfort.

+

feral exists at that fiendish intersection of gender, race, and class. feral girls can teach ourselves how to english. we are good mimics, savvy code-switchers. most working-class girls are far more dexterous than boys at pin-balling back and forth between restricted and elaborated modes of speech and the social roles that engender them. we will often have a "school voice", a "home voice" and a "street corner voice". it gives us a bit of superficial social mobility, but it also drives us to daily acts of self-induced schizophrenia: multiple improvised and competing performances. boys don't deal with the pressure of that on anything like the same level as girls. you can be a working-class male and still embody some form of exemplary masculinity; there are more permissible *ways to be* male. working-class girls are not models of exemplary femininity. not ever. we're too loud, too coarse. as we grow, the things we're trained to minimise about our class background contribute to our oppression *as* women. well-behaved girls don't push themselves forward. nice girls are modest and well-mannered. to be thought of as "well brought up" is to defer in discussion, submissive and fawning. if not, we are considered deserving of rough treatment and ultimately disposable. we can be "beautiful" of course, but beauty isn't power, not really, not the power to *do* anything, not to move or to think, but to passively attract, to benefit from the dubious boon of male attention. we can't win. we're branded by the signifiers we fail to shake; we're not women in any meaningful sense, we're punchlines, comic strips, stereotypes. and if that's all we are, they don't have to scruple over how we are treated. feral has seen her future: bruised and wearied, tending bar, gawped at and groped on for minimum wage. it's not the job itself. she could work as a stripper or a checkout operator and the situation would be the same. her labour exposes her, true, but it's her *innate* lack of worth that renders her fair game for male predation. there's no level of respect, protection, or redress that she's entitled to. if she kicks herself free from her class background, wriggling out of the wet, rubberised skin of poverty, she's no better off. she nices herself to eclipse. she's one of those tiny, darting fish, swimming in the slipstream of a shark. one of those thin, spindly birds riding along on a crocodile's back. she is only ever protected from male violence by travelling in the wake of male violence. she is appealing and useful, says "please" and "thank you"; she has fluffy words for candyfloss ideas. language determines and constitutes our intellectual operations. duh. it isn't merely a medium of expression, it shapes what *can* be thought, everything it's possible to frame and know. if it's not ladylike to shout or swear or interrupt; if we can't name the places in ourselves that hurt, broach the ways in which we are hurt, how can we ever defend ourselves, define our own realities? we're not given the words in which to rage. all language is an imperfect compromise with lived experience, but what can we make or understand with breathy euphemisms, whispers, polite little obfuscations? occupying forces will always prohibit and punish use of the native language. it was so in ireland in 1690, in 1916, and in 1984 when prison authorities forbid the speaking of gaelic in long kesh because irish itself was deemed "sectarian", irrespective of what was being said. an insurrectionary pressure builds at the back of a common tongue. you speak yourself into resistance; your language holds you, gives you strength. to force your thoughts through the tongue of another is to find them stunted, stuttering; diminished and divided. this applies as much to grammar as the language itself. my speech is "vulgar", "rude". i must learn to be equivocal and vacillating, to root out all my splendid, earthy negations. don't say "fuck off!" don't even say "no!" don't contradict, refuse, or hold to account. use english words, succinct sentences, absolute restraint. that's how girls talk. to succeed at "girl" is to dig the splintery verbal of home from your mouth, pulling your teeth out with pliers to make more room for "pleasant" and for "feminine". language is the doing of class, culture, and community. "girl" is a censorship, the erasure of those things from speech, her gender is her only country.

+

feral child. i heard that a lot. i read that a lot. it's fear, isn't it? fear of what "feral" does to "child", how it cancels out or makes strange the category of "child", where "child" is something innocent, both cosseted and free from care. what manner of creature could thrive in a feral environment? their survival is obscene. they 'fatten on offal'. so "feral" *must* be made to cancel "child", is a functional denial of "child". if not, how to sleep with what we do to children, poor children, black children, brown children, traveller children? refugee children? "feral" is an elastic word; it is an innate quality and a perverse choice. the "feral child" is predisposed to delinquent behaviour. her wayward nature is a cause in itself. it is not the result of social conditions, and nobody need feel responsible to or for her. yet the "feral child" is feral on purpose. unlike the humbly suffering stray, she rejects the normalising aspirations of her betters and bites the hand that feeds her. she will not be helped, so we do not have to help her. she threatens us, so we do not have to acknowledge her vulnerability, or all the ways in which *she* is threatened.

+

their "feral" refused my vulnerability, so my feral becomes a swaggering synanthrope, superbly adapted. i am grasping feral like a young, green nettle. i am not letting go. if i cover myself and cringe, then it isn't from shame, but a defence against disgust and its consequences. i'm not ashamed. i am not *really* afraid. if they want feral, i will fight them for it. my feral is not an extension of their gutless deterministic tropes: where the female body is closer to nature, allied to the land, to its rhythms and cycles; instinctive and nurturing, endlessly fertile. my feral wants none. if the male body is the site and source of expertise; of power, rationality, and technical control, then that makes women something to be dominated, colonised, exploited, and consumed. fuck that noise. my feral knows that if women are nature, then poor women are nature in its most abject aspect. then poor women are only nature in the sense that nature itself is: a) a tool. b) a currency. c) a resource. d) a surplus. e) a waste. if feral is evicted from the feminine, she will return the feminine to sender, exaggerated and burlesqued. feral is all or nothing: her sexuality is menacing, absent to fantasy. it is too much. it is absolute zero. irrational, renunciate. feral unmakes herself. would sooner have revulsion than desire. understands that both will be weaponised to bring her to heel. feral is a fugitive. feral is a fighter. she will go down swinging. don't say *survivor*, where survival becomes some cheesy obligation to joy. to be ashamed of being victimised, as if *that* were a choice, as if survival were a state and not a process. there are no *survivors*, only surviv*ing*, and all of us are or none of us are.

POUNDLAND ACADEMIC VERSUS THE RAINBOW CAPITALIST BORG

"poundland academic" is not my phrase, but it is a phrase that has been applied to me, and it has come to be a label i revel in and relish. when i use this phrase about myself, the assumption tends to be that i do so in a self-deprecating way, or that i have internalised the negative stereotyping that circumscribes the experience of poor others inside of academia. but that's not the case. "poundland academic" is not a critical assessment of my intellectual capacities *or* the quality and rigour of my research. rather, it is a comment on how those things are interpreted, misinterpreted (in ways both deliberate and unconscious), and framed by the academy. when the label is applied to me from the outside the implications are *not* positive: they turn on a fundamental misunderstanding of Poundland as synonymous with imitative shoddiness. it's not merely that the goods themselves are cheap and lacking in value, it is that they incompetently ape "genuine" quality brands. as an insult "poundland academic" is predicated on the assumption that as a working-class person my participation in the academy can only ever be imitative and incompetent; i can originate neither knowledge nor the research methodologies by which new knowledge is produced; my work must always be either derivative or low-key fraudulent. usually both. it is also an insult that conflates my research with my embodied presence as a poor working-class other; reading my "bad" aesthetic and presentational "choices" as synonymous with or symbolic of my intellectual abilities.

+

but Poundland – however else you feel about its business model – is not solely driven by a bargain-basement imitation of more expensive and better-quality brands (although this is definitely an element of the store's money-spinning strategy). Poundland also carries clearance and seasonal stock, often from proprietary products. it keeps prices low by buying in bulk, and by offering an ever-changing array of end-of-line deals. while the branding on some of its products does tread perilously close to copyright infringement, it is not – contrary to middle-class misconception – that customers are "fooled" by this surface similarity, or indeed that they intend to fool others. on one level at least it is more obvious and more basic than that: if you've no money, and two products are functionally and aesthetically identical, why wouldn't you pick the cheaper of the two? in some instances the less expensive doppelgänger is an inferior version of its premium-priced twin (the astringent aroma of Poundland's yankee-looking scented candles could strip paint, and their "fake kenco" coffee tastes like burnt gravy) but mostly a bourbon biscuit is a bourbon biscuit, washing-up liquid is washing-up liquid, and baked beans – regardless of what breathy M&S adverts tell you – are baked fecking beans. it's not complicated: poor people want to buy products that are as appealingly packaged as those aimed at their more affluent contemporaries.

+

all of which is to say that what characterises Poundland is not imitation at all, but the arbitrary and the opportunistic, the often baffling and seemingly random range of products on offer (i once found a hardback copy of Aleksandr Solzhenitsyn's *the red wheel* in there). what defines Poundland is that special element of instability and chance which dominates poor and working-class retail experience. one literally cannot afford to be choosy; our straitened economic condition requires and encourages a high degree of adaptability and improvisation. these are also the qualities that characterise working-class intellectual engagement. certainly, they are the qualities that exemplify my own best research, work that embraces modes of opportunistic scavenging, workaround, make-do, recycling and riff to uncover knowledge unavailable to traditional research methodologies. the idea of *riff* is significant, as distinct from mere imitation: *riff* is a subtly destabilising variation incorporating burlesque or parody towards the ends of criticism and change. *riff* is pun, embellishment, is mad hyperbolic play. *riff* is intentional and ironising. it is to wallow, to revel, to turn the dials up to eleven on the fakeness of the fake, so that fakeness itself becomes a mode and a commentary. exaggerating the stylistic tropes and tendencies of middle-class consumer culture distorts the pristine, impenetrable aura of their referential power. the symbols of consumer status are not aped but undermined. this is not just a debased performance of value, *this* is an interrogation of "value" and the unequal power dynamics that construct and maintain it as a category.

+

we're not *doing* you in order to become you. our doing undoes you. and if we are "failing" we are failing with purpose and/or on purpose. as Anahid Nersessian writes of Keats, and his use of catachresis, his intention is to: 'acclaim life's capacity to defy its forcible metamorphosis, and to do so by pitting rhetorical misuse against economic abuse [...] catachresis cuts at least three ways. it is a positive dereliction, a winning effort at going against the grain; it is a mistake; and in any case it is a disturbance, even, as some commentators suggest, an act of violence or an offering of injury' (2020). in other words, Keats, in all his hyperbolic excess, deploys inelegance and misuse (of language, syntax, and grammar) as a tool to broach social criticism and reinvent poetic method. this method is predicated upon a poetics of "failure", but perhaps all poetry is a form of failure. and isn't that something of what Aimé Césaire meant when he wrote: 'la connaissance poétique naît dans la grand silence de la connaissance scientifique' or 'poetic knowledge is born in the silence of scientific knowledge' (1945)? which is to say, poetry can access ways of knowing untouched by instrumental rationality. there's a specific anticolonial context here: poetry is aligned with the desires, expressions, and possibilities of a free humanity, while science is an agent of conquest and control. In this formulation there's a promise that poetry might wrest or wrestle language away from dominant meaning systems, that it might open up new forms of perception and social relation. And not in "succeeding" by the inherited standards, aims, and trajectories of "high" art and culture, but in radically and wilfully failing them.

+

this idea has huge implications for the working-class other inside of the academy, where the pressure to conform to, even to surpass, middle-class expectations and standards is excruciating. a phrase i hear a lot from my working-class colleagues is "working twice as hard to be thought of as half as good". i've said it before and i'll say it again: privilege isn't about "knowing the rules", it is never having to learn them in the first place. rules are for the others, for whom there are no shortcuts, for whom there is no benefit of the doubt, whose diligence, talent, and expertise will never be taken for granted, whose diligence, talent, and expertise will, in fact, be subjected to pitiless scrutiny at every step. poor and working-class academics struggle to meet the unequal demands of exceptionalism placed upon them by a system that fails to recognise material disparity and its domino effects on time, energy, and attention. further, it is a system singularly blind to the extra invisible labour involved in fast-mapping all of those rules; to the bobbing and weaving required to negotiate institutions and logics set up to exclude you. so much of the other's ability to inhabit elite literary and intellectual space is contingent upon "passing": on concealing or minimising the aspects of ourselves that impede the smooth functioning of culture, the confirmation of status, and the transfer of knowledge. the space of the page within print and publication cultures often works to eradicate difference through standardised typography, lineation, and an insistence – for example – on "correct" spelling, grammar, and "good" prosody. feral must interest itself in what happens when the mask slips, the performance stutters, or is refused altogether. can incompetence, ugliness, tonal inconsistency, all of that Keatsian misuse, be deployed as a tool to destabilise and reinvigorate poetic or intellectual method?

+

something else i hear a lot from my poor and working-class peers is the phrase "fighting on two fronts". this refers not only to our manic oscillation between two wildly adverse sets of cultural and social expectations, inside the academy and out, but to the doubly defensive nature of – on the one hand – striving for recognition of what we do as legitimate and valuable within our own families and cohorts, and – on the other – struggling to secure some acknowledgement of the socioeconomic conditions in which we live and work from the institutions that employ us. on the rare occasions this last is forthcoming it is subject to a hideous catch-22 whereby the acknowledgement of poverty serves only to reinforce an idea of the working-class academic as deficient and failing. in this scenario, poverty itself is treated as a catchword or "card", one tied to an overt performance of working-class "identity" and cynically exploited to fraudulently secure support or excuse a lack of intellectual rigour. to put it more plainly: to be accepted and acknowledged as poor and working-class, you are expected to perform your working-classness in accordance with a limited set of tropes characterised by suffering, deficiency, victimisation, and want. such performances construct "working-class" as a monolithic and unassailable identity category, excluding those who are not comfortably cradled within its prescribed parameters. and yet the very existence of this category is used to deny our work legitimacy. we did not create it, we cannot control it. the system's sewn up. we were born to lose, set-up to fail.

+

unless. unless we no longer choose to measure "success" on their terms. unless we decide we are done with "success" altogether. unless, like the anecdotal chess-playing chicken, we don't compete with our oppressors, but kick over the pieces, shit on the board, and strut around as if we've won. "poundland academics" will jam and mangle, they will spite the inherited notion of status contained within the practice of arts and culture, and they are *not* interested in the aims of instrumental eloquence or mastery. they are, in fact, feral.

+

the chicken is not the target of that joke. you might think she is, but she's not. she can't be. she isn't subject to the logics of the game to begin with. she can't "win" by shitting and strutting, but she can't meaningfully "lose" either, because neither of those words, nor the meaning-systems that produced them, are relevant to her experience of the world. the chicken is our hero. she is gleefully indifferent. the loser in that analogy is the petit Ahab attempting to prove their mastery over an animal by subjecting her to the limited metrics of human judgement. don't get excited, but i've invoked the chicken for a reason, as an exemplar of the "dumb animal", where "dumb" is used to equate silence with "stupidity". of the animal industrial complex's many casualties, chickens, i think, fare worst. constructed by western culture as "naturally" expendable and forgettable, they are consistently framed as mere utility stock, to the extent that language makes no effort to conceal the animal behind the meat, to spare our ethical blushes by transforming her into an absent referent. no, 'chicken' refers both to the living animal and to her flesh. this over-determination of chickens as mere food even while alive contributes to their maltreatment and trivialisation as a species. even within discourses that theorise animal sentience and advocate for non-human personhood, chickens function solely as a comparison to those animals (whales, dolphins, chimpanzees) that demonstrate the consciousness and mental ingenuity upon which basis rights ought to be awarded. a related and equally insidious strand of thought suggests that farm animals being 'bred to docility, tractability, stupidity, and dependency' as mere 'creations of man' are exempt from the category of the "natural" that affords their wild cousins the smallest morsel of moral consideration (1980). funny, isn't it? by which i mean screamingly frustrating. that those animal qualities deemed to confer a modicum of ethical considerability are the very qualities with which heterosexual men have traditionally identified, admired, and sought to emulate, even as they pit themselves against, subjugate, and destroy those same animals? (Karen Davis, 1995). the qualities of "stupidity and dependency" on the other hand, have been naturalised as belonging to women, forming the logical basis (and the justification) for their historic mistreatment and oppression.

+

but "stupidity" is far from being an innate characteristic. it is, rather, a construct that society both punishes and naturalises in women, and denies (or recuperates as charming vulnerability) in straight white men. Halberstam suggests that male stupidity is the goofy grin that masks the will to power; that it masquerades as the fulfilment of feminist critique (clueless male requires omni-competent female badass to educate and civilise him), which in turn conceals the inequality that structures male-female relationships. and yet, stupidity and failure also offer a means of resistance, can be productive of: 'a certain kind of absence—the absence of memory or the absence of wisdom— [that] leads to a new form of knowing. stupidity conventionally means different things in relation to different subject positions; for example, stupidity in white men can signify new modes of domination, but stupidity in women of all ethnicities inevitably symbolises their status as, in psychoanalytic terms, "castrated" or impaired. in relation to the theme of productive failure, stupidity and forgetfulness work hand in hand to open up new and different ways of being in relation to time, truth, being, living, and dying. […]' (2011). what the world calls "stupidity" can, in fact, function as a space of non-rational relation in which the continuous inscription of hierarchy can be fruitfully disrupted. i mean, why would we denigrate impaired function when "functionality" itself is geared towards producing such horrible, life-denying results? the smooth and malignant operation of the late-capitalist death machine. in other words: be more chicken.

+

or not. but it is worth concerning ourselves with "stupid" forms of cultural production: with the disavowed and disreputable, with slapstick and schlock, with the queasy, cringeworthy, necrotised kitsch of queer style. how classed, gendered, and racialised is, for example, our notion of prosody, and what makes "good" art, "good" literature, "good" taste? let's consider the exclamation mark, with all its thrillingly ambiguous expressive effects; an over-the-topness that conveys both volume and intensity. a shout. a slap. it's tabloidy, unprofessional, a kind of gutter punctuation. it belongs to popular culture, it's tacky, proletarian, and camp. a typographical hyena that no one knows how to read: a threat? a warning? a joyous whoop? but where in elite literary space is it allowed to live? here's some snobbery for you: 'except in poetry the exclamation mark should be used sparingly. excessive use of exclamation marks in expository prose is a sure sign of an unpractised writer or of one who wants to add a spurious dash of sensation to something unsensational.' from *fowler's modern english usage.* or, my absolute favourite: 'so far as good writing goes, the use of the exclamation mark is a sign of failure. it is the literary equivalent of a man holding up a card reading "laughter" to a studio audience.' from Miles Kingston, writing in *punch.*

+

seeing as how poetry and comedy have been dragged into this, let's consider poetry and comedy: undervalued/devalued (feral) within the cultural hierarchies that ascribe relevance and worth to aesthetic modes. to quote from Maggie Hennefeld and Nicholas Sammond, comedy in particular – 'no matter how graphically violent, offensively crude, or vividly grotesque – has the power to present even the most disturbing content as entirely unserious' (2020). or, to quote from Lauren Berlant 'comedy's action pro-duces anxiety: risking transgression, flirting with displeasure, or just confusing things in a way that intensifies and impedes the pleasure.' in other words, comedy is not reducible to an escapist flight from the traumas of brutal reality, rather 'as comedy expands to encompass the anxious and horrible, it signals the abjecting of a tidy poetics of being, of anything ever again being "just a joke."'

(2017). stupidity in its purest form has a weird transformative power, can render the familiar uncanny, can dwell in such extreme detail or approach from such counter-intuitive tangents that our most cherished ideas become strange or disgusting to us. this unsettling shift in perspective is something that *both* poetry and comedy excel at. both – to riff on Andrei Codrescu – 'sabotage the narratives of Archives in ways that would allow the Archives of Amnesia to pour through into the present.' (2013).

+

by 'Archives of Amnesia' Codrescu signals the 'history of vanquished', a history that exists only in its erasure, that is written out of the official archives. he considers that a straightforward telling of this history might in itself constitute a recapitulation of the violence inflicted by the initial erasure because of the 'inevitable anger, horror, and helplessness that follows the restoration.' restoration isn't repair, ken? instead, Codrescu states that forgetting is 'more important an art than total recall. amnesia shapes the few remembered or misremembered scenes into whatever you're going to make. the kind of remembering that interests me is anamnesis, which is an intense flashback. such a flashback is generally devoid of facts because it has room only for feeling'. anamnesis is the involuntary revival of memory provoked by a particular signal – a sound or a word out of place – it is surprising, disorienting; it cannot be mastered, disciplined, or trained to walk at heel. it is not amenable to rationality, it will not conform to orderly linear narrative habits. it dwells in the distraction, the glitch, the segue, the ramble, the lame-brained misread, the error, the inappropriate guffaw, the awkward silence, the tumbleweed dad joke; in registers of ostentatious self-ridicule, gathering nervous laughter to itself in the form of queer affirmation.

+

which is great. except the systems inside of which we labour are continually trying to assimilate or exclude this laughter. often both. simultaneously. through the creation of multiple categories and tropes. for example, the scholarly figure of "emergence", which can be used to conjure the vanguard or cutting edge, but is, more often, slyly deployed as an infantilising temporality that communicates (and contributes to) perpetual marginalisation. an emergent field or artist is always on the verge of becoming – unfinished, not yet stable or perfected – but it may never "arrive". or again, the category of the "outsider artist", that sneaky little act of semantic subordination that recuperates, even as it excludes, the difficult art made by social others back into establishment discourse. "outsider artist" functions as a way of claiming this art while keeping the others who produce it at arm's length, positioning them as backward and inferior. it allows middle-class critics to nod to, without ever having to fully credit, the rich, aesthetic basis of the art made by others. "outsider art" frames features as bugs, and choices as accidents of untutored energy, preserving the myth that rigour and innovation are solely the fruits of middle-class literary and artistic production.

+

elites need these tactics. they need them because the middle classes are not, in fact, fearless originators of new knowledge and culture, but hopelessly insecure and imitative, feeding alike on the mores and social habits of the rich, and the art, style, and energy of the poor. there is a middle-class discourse for any working-class subculture you care to name. we are mediated, packaged and repackaged, displaced, replaced, sold back to ourselves. case in point: punk. case in point: "retro".

+

in recent years retro has been frigging everywhere, a stylistic expression of the weaponised nostalgia mobilised by the tories during brexit and the last general election. retro is not the same as the anachronistic borrowings made by – say – punks, rudeboys and mods. it is, rather, neoliberal culture's way of reabsorbing and recolonising the past, of forcing our avenues of exploration and adventure back into an inescapable circuit with a rotten present. retro narrows the past into a series of easily identifiable, consumer-friendly images; these images are then ripe for mass production. retro is copy-paste and shop-bought. it removes any element of archaeology or investigation from the process of creating style. it replaces style with a shallow array of disembodied and impersonal "looks". all surface, taken in at a glance. retro shears the past of its textures, subtleties, and secrets, its unique political and historical context. while the original drive towards retro fashions in the nineteen sixties could be seen as critical of consumer culture – restraining demand for new products and reusing the old in defiance of capitalist relations – the borg eventually assimilated retro into its operating logics, launching a series of less durable and infinitely more expensive replicas. or, if clothes are not new, they are "vintage", that is, endorsed by and welcomed into the new, with a price tag to match. in the world of retro there are no human beings. we don't have to think about the bodies that previously occupied these clothes, or consider ourselves as part of a strange, dislocated lineage. we don't have to acknowledge the working-class invention that created the style, of the pressured innovation that drove its evolution. in the world of retro there are no classes. retro is for those who have the luxury of forgetting the past, their own past and that of the world. retro is a past without accessing memory. the working-class subject is tied to *their* past. we drag it behind us like a withered limb. this warm-blooded heaviness is part, for me, of *doing* punk: our second-hand, shoplifted clothes had been customised to death. our battle jackets and boots accumulated and stored the scars of lived experience, became a tactile repository, an archive of our own, whose lives were defined by the ephemeral, precarious, and impermanent. we wanted something we could carry, who did not have the security of solid walls around us. by the late nineties punk was dead, but that was half the point. as Cynthia Cruz writes 'this insistence on the past drags it into the present, creating a glitch in the system' (2021). and this is a deeply serious form of resistance-play: resistance to disposable culture. to the idea of ourselves as disposable. to the sinister and perpetually questing cool-hunt of late-stage capitalism, its malignant rapidity, its capacious swallow. we liked to think that we opened for ourselves and each other a parallel timeline. punk's aims had never been realised, its demands never met, our lives had never improved for all of its thrashing and screaming. so, we rededicated ourselves, we made of our bodies and our persons a last anachronistic redoubt. punk is – in its truest form – the unquantifiable part of style indigestible as (to) fashion. punk is feral. a synanthropic and liminal species. an unforgiving-edgelands animal. i modelled my own mohawk haircut on the striped hyena's mane.

+

the edge can be a lonely and difficult place. we tell ourselves our vulnerability is the price we pay for freedom, but such "freedom" is far from secured. *sparks fly at the edge.* this is the outcast's consolation. and yet, even as they keep you at arm's length, they fold the fruits of that frustrated industry back into their dully functioning centre; use it to refresh and sustain themselves. it is a very particular species of theft, not only the appropriation of techniques or themes, but the cynical misdirection of effort and energy: *you* are the allegorical catfish in the cod tank. you keep them just agile and alert enough to stay alive. while the uniquely pressured position of the feraltern subject drives her relentless innovation, rarely will she receive recognition or reward for the same. rather, her work will be mediated, interpreted, and ultimately metabolised into myriad crowd-pleasing imitations. *this* work will come to overwrite and replace her difficult original, so much so that it will, after a time, define what it means to make art in the manner of *x*, a category from which our feraltern artist-subject is now effectively excluded. it is not, as has so often been suggested, imitation as the sincerest form of value-neutral flattery. rather, it is a process of assimilation, replication and replacement, a process that is only made possible through the dynamics of hierarchy and suppression that operate between the centre and the edge. lemme give you a big obvious for instance: Elvis Presley was not flattering Big Mama Thornton when he took the alabama singer's hymn to black female empowerment ('hound dog') for his own. his very success, his very visibility, as an exceptional white, male artist, is predicated on her relative obscurity, on forcing her back to the margins. the song, written specifically for her, to fit her often animalised embodied presence as a large, scarred, working-class black woman, is shorn of its history and context in the slick Presley version. Presley is often credited as a champion of black music, for bringing black musical culture to the (white, middle-american) mainstream. but acculturation's logics are always those of absorption and merger, and this frame of reference is in itself deeply problematic, inscribing the power differential it claims to be usefully undermining, asserting that the value of black music lies in its capacity to enrich white music and to be appreciated by white audiences. it also claims that black aesthetic and performative traditions require mediation and reinterpretation by white ambassadors to render them legible, accessible, acceptable. indeed, it's most blinkered assumption would seem to be that this accessibility is something black musicians would want in the first place.

+

okay. so, music is the most easily observable example of this trend because of its broad populist appeal, but it happens across all of art and literature. in poetry, the problem is compounded by the fact that feraltern art and its pod-poem replacements may appear on the page as indistinguishable to the naked eye. what is the difference, for example, between a piece of work in which a major (hegemonic) language like english is deterritorialised by inserting into it words, phrases, and structures from a subaltern or marginalised language, and a piece of work in which the language of the feraltern other is pillaged to spice and nourish that same hegemonic language? or, to put it another way: how do you spot a fake? especially if it's a good fake? especially if the priest-class of critics responsible for adjudicating upon a work, generating the discourse surrounding it, and interpreting it to its readership have a vested interest in perpetuating the fraud?

+

fun fact: your agent (urgh) does not love you. your publisher, in all likelihood, does not love you. their ideal artist is a tragic death (preferably suicide) with an insanely prolific body of work behind them, and to which they have secured the rights. they do not want your living body, but its functional ghost, the faked punk of your beautiful ruin. you live in a world and a publishing culture where even your death – especially your death – can be recruited as a unique selling point. people love a dead iconoclast. and of course, there is a date-stamp on their iconoclasm, they may safely indulge its legend, separate from the active political forms of its expression: Che Guevara, Sid Vicious, Sylvia Plath,

Sean Bonney. it *looks* like zeitgeist. it is, in fact, nostalgia.

+

worse than any of this: i have become a false flag made of myself. institutions wave me from their battlements, and the call goes forth that this is a "safe", "inclusive" space, here's the proof. i'm the proof. but it's not "safe". i don't feel "safe". my heart is so heavy.

+

sometimes you have to wonder if it isn't the operating logics of the entire set-up that eventually destroy people. peak fucking *gadjo*. which is not to say that individual contracts are exploitative or that individual publishers are "bad". i think what i am actually talking about is the fraught meeting between two incommensurable value systems. not that the offer of legally binding exclusivity is "unfair" as much as "fairness" itself is not something that signifies beyond their moderate, liberal framework. it's that the contract at all is an ominous metaphor for – and fragment of – a political-legal world of liberal citizenship of which you are justifiably wary and *in* which you have no real stake. it isn't as trite as *freedom means more to me than money*. it's that *freedom* means differently to you. the contract makes you feel pressured, pursued, cornered, forced. it is an extension of a world in which you are exhaustively administered. a world that begrudges and punishes you, that expects you to be grateful. in this world, to sign is to concede; to enter into any "deal" entails a loss. you know this in your bones. this otherness they all make so much of is not an identity category. it impacts the way you relate and move through the deep structures that underpin everything we do. poetry's especially odd: it wants to marketise otherness in the form of consumable art, but it does a bad job of recognising and extending care to the othered subject producing that art. it likes the representational triumph of visible forms of difference, but it doesn't want to think about what this difference does to how we access and navigate the infrastructures they take for granted. as in, infrastructure *is* entrapment genius. resources to be withheld or maimed, according to the logics of sovereignty. which reserves the right, not only to produce the wound, but to refuse, in short order, protection, repair, or redress. this is not abstract. the poor – the other – live under occupation.

+

we can be terribly naïve: we like to think that those who profess to care about the work will naturally be invested in the well-being of the body and brain that produced it. nine times out of ten that isn't the case. when was the last time *you* were referred to as "a machine"? a phrase that emerges disguised as a compliment, but that betrays the extent to which others are willing to deny you your personhood. of course, you *are* prolific, but invisiblised inside "prolific" is the sweat, the effort, the unequal labour, the endless tedious shitwork. "prolific" functions as a refusal of the anxiety and disparity that drives being so. if the work is both a psychological compulsion and a practical necessity, then both of these things are intimately tied to your experiences as classed, gendered, and racialised subjects; to the times you have been called lazy or incapable, told that your life only has value if instrumentalised in the service of something greater than your lowly self. "prolific" disappears the hardwired imperative to be incessantly producing, from *having* to produce in order to maintain a presence, to meaningfully "compete". to be shy, retiring, slow and considered, all of these luxuries you cannot afford. the feraltern subject will simply not get away with farting out one wafer thin book every three years or so and expecting to have it feted (ahem). "prolific" excites jealous comment or *sotto voce* whispers on the subject of obnoxious self-promotion from the arbiters of a social etiquette that disproportionately favours the privileged. you will be told that you are "lucky" to be "able" to produce so much by those who miss that terrible, imperative summons. and from those who are supported and maintained in the creation of their art. and yes, of course there is a plus side: persistent innovation, constant surprise, ruptures that become pathways opening up all over the shop within feral practice. but it also means that we over-extend to the point of exhaustion, that we live with a constant gnawing dread, an endless obligation to *do*.

+

within elite academe this psychological stress is fed by the very real, systemic pressures of REF (that is, research excellence framework), the mechanism by which staff "contributions" to the academy are measured and assessed. are you an asset to the university? what prizes have you won? what research have you published? and in which journals? REF absolutely fails to account for the unique conditions under which creative practitioners labour, or to acknowledge that there's an entirely different set of metrics at play in the acceptance and publication of creative work than for pure research. the rhythms of creative publication are also different: unpredictable and slow, often pretty fucking arbitrary; they are subject to last minute cancellation or change, they are dependent on the whims of a rotating cast of editors, sub-editors, and sensitivity readers. in no other field is work rejected simply because it doesn't "sing" or thrill. so, what do you do? sideline the creative component of your research, allow yourself to be edited out of creative and cultural space so that the thing you love can be effectively colonised by economic and social elites? tricky. and doesn't tory britain attach such absolute and unassailable moral authority to the notion of "hard work" and to being "hard working"? such shame is inculcated in you as a working-class person for being thought of as a member of the "undeserving poor" that you excoriate yourself for failing in your obligation to joyless slog, and this in a climate in which full employment is – one more time with feeling – quite *literally* impossible. it's buried so deeply: socially inscribed, culturally and semantically hard-wired. we say "working-class" and so much is encoded in that phrase, it carries so many layered associations. queer woman at desk, writing poetry, thinking thoughts, is definitely not one of them. and academia doesn't get it. its collective embrace of the nauseating "do what you love" mantra has led to the devaluation of work and the denigration of workers. if we take the exhortation to "do what we love" at face value, then we skew our conception of labour from something we do for financial compensation towards an act self-betterment, of pure unadulterated joygasm. in this scenario, our inability to derive either profit or pleasure from what we do is a moral failure, a deficiency of passion and energy. *we* are to blame, not the pressured, precarious position in which we find ourselves. in all, it's a nasty little maxim, one designed to hoodwink us into believing that labour serves individual psychological fulfilment and not the global market-place. *no*where is this more prevalent or explicit than inside the academy, where what we do – our research, our creative practice, our teaching obligations – are assumed to be undertaken from a swooning surplus of sheer love. it becomes anathema to complain, to speak of it as work, to acknowledge the actual conditions and compensations of our labour at all. but coming from poverty you cannot help but acknowledge them, you obsess over them, over all the hair-trigger calibrations of time and finance that govern your every day. you can't afford to buy into "do what you love", on a zero-hours contract, with no benefits, no job security, ridiculously long and unsociable hours, with no real stake in the institutions for which you toil. yet this doctrine is absolutely ingrained in academia, fusing personal identity with work output so completely and intimately, that to disagree is to be alienated. in every sense.

+

what can feral do to break this masochistic pact? especially when her work exhausts her. her work exhausts her for the work of her work. her work *is* exhaustion, that is 'expenditure'. what is left of her for the structures inside of which she toils, that demand she *use* that which her work can only *spend*? must feral disappear? fade, wear out, resign, collapse? no!

ON 'RENARDIE'
(FOX PROBLEMS, FOX PIVOTS)

i was thinking about foxes. i had been watching a dead fox decay for weeks. the gashed mouth appeared first agonised, then leering, then a mere complacent hinge. the fox came apart as the weather turned: loose divots of soiled fur, a diaspora of bones. one morning the dog sniffed out her skull, rolled into a furrow on the ploughed-up field. the teeth were white, astonishingly so, except for a brown remnant of *something* caught in a cavity. i lifted the skull with a stick and hung her in the hawthorn. i had used to boil and bleach the animal skulls i found in the field, but for fox this did not feel right. in any case, a village neighbour waxed about parasites. bones, which had always seemed to me so hauntingly void, were, in reality, teemingly tenanted. alive with their own inscrutable ecology. i walked home troubled, thinking about foxes. it was wanting to honour fox. or, not *honour*, because what could that mean to fox? but *witness*. there was an intimacy and obscure privilege in marking, day by day, the slow progress of her dissolution. it was, of course, all we could be said to share. i wanted to meet her in the starkness of it. neither beautiful nor abject, not even truly sad. merely inevitable.

+

on my walk i listen to birdsong. or sometimes i listen to podcasts. sometimes the human voices say things that make me deeply angry. on this occasion it is about the dead. the exceptional, suicided dead who "died too young". *too young for what?* i scowl at the scum on a frozen puddle as i break it with my boot. as if it were fair to hold a body that had opted out to the promissory logics of supply and demand. what they might have *achieved*, what they might have *accomplished*. as if a fruitfully producing life were the absolute measure of worth; its loss the absolute measure of tragedy. what a *waste*, they say, conflating the loss of that life with the loss of the work, until that person is disappeared completely inside of their output. i hate this language. as much in its implications for the living as for the dead. if the termination of artistic productivity is some kind of catastrophic *waste*, then what does that mean for those who outlive their creative energies? the flip-side to "they died too young" is that *you*, old crone, surplus eater, have lived too late. unlike the dead, those of us who survive the diminishment of artistic power, sexual vitality, and cultural cachet are not available for recuperation inside of a system that wants nothing more than to monetise your dead self as a crowd-pleasing fetish in the cult of doomed exceptionalism. i walk along thinking about foxes. and hounds. about the instrumental quality of our animal attachments. round here they cull deer, they cull foxes, cull badgers, cull rabbits. there are too many of them, they're "upsetting the balance", and what have they done for *us* lately? walking and walking, all the hedgerows of enclosure, where "balance" is that which benefits human beings. how much of a stake does an animal have in her environment? are we so sure that the governing principle of nature is "balance" at all? and not wild oscillation, pivot and flux? "balance" is a lie to valorise what serves us under the guise of responsible stewardship. we're not so concerned with harmonious equilibrium when *we* are its disruptors. ask the forest cleared for grazing. ask the fistulated cow. ask the roadkill, the monocrop, the bees poisoned by pesticides. they apply this double standard to the poor too. such an eyesore we are, our sites, our estates. we're a "burden on society", a "strain on resources", a "blot on the landscape". they adjudicate on the value of our lives according to the extent we are seen to "contribute". and they get to decide what constitutes a "contribution" in the first place.

thinking about foxes. some of my favourite therianthropic witch legends centre around women who would turn themselves into foxes to lead a hunt astray. i have long been obsessed by the magical transformation of people into animals, from the times my own body felt strange and dangerous to me, either through pain, or through mental illness, when i was changing my body in ways both involuntary and conscious. the magnitude of my feelings demanded and drove these changes, a remaking and remapping at the physical level. all of my "normal" bodily functions suspended, caught in arrest or revolt outside the rational flow of time. anorexia felt disciplined and vigilant, a charm, a hex, a magic "working". the opposite of *death-wish*, it was violently survivalist. i drained myself of "erotic capital", rendered myself unfit for work: domestic, emotional, sexual. i wanted to be of zero utility to their world. it was a scorched earth policy enacted against and through the self. shapeshift. shed the human suit. my weight dropped so low that i grew a fine down of hair across my body. i could trace my spine, prominent, like some vestigial tail. my gums bled, my period stopped. therianthropy: my animal transformation. there were not enough words and not the right words and too many words to make sense, so i recruited the body, resorted to gesture, emptied myself and entered the animal. of course, witches were foxes. most witches were elderly, indigent women, a continuous and obtruding presence in the streets of their local communities, begging for food, for milk, for alms. an accusation of witchcraft was a mechanism of social cleansing, either to expunge the powerless, or to remove those who seemed on the cusp of claiming power. Silvia Federici tells us that a belief in magic was a huge stumbling block to the rationalisation of the work process. it functioned as a form of feral refusal, of insubordination and grass-roots resistance. women's claim to magical power undermined state authority; it gave the poor and powerless hope that they could manipulate and control the natural environment, and by extension subvert the social order (2004). of course, witches were foxes. a fox "contributes" neither meat nor labour. it does not make a present from the heat-sealed wallet of itself. it cannot be put to work. it takes without thanks, it has nothing tangible to trade, it cannot be reduced to an unwitting partner in a swindlers bargain.

+

dead fox, disarticulated paw, off-white like a scrimshawed fork. even the language of animal rights has been miserably reduced. i read that while the annual cost of fox predation on poultry and livestock is estimated at around £10–12 million, the benefit of foxes to arable farmers in keeping down rabbit populations has been calculated at around £7–9 million. it is also argued that they aid commercial forestry by predating species that damage young trees, and that culling foxes has no effect on fox populations at all, other than locally. if numbers are suppressed more cubs are born the following spring. there is *no* evidence that fox numbers have significantly increased since the ban on hunting in 2005. good arguments, i suppose, but appealing to a certain kind of logic, a certain kind of mind: "reasonable", "rational". our village neighbour doesn't believe in hunting with dogs, of course, any more than he believes in animal vivisection "where there is an alternative", any more than he believes in deforestation "more than is necessary". oh yes, everything global capitalism dominates must perforce be classified and controlled in order to be managed. we protect what is marketable, and nature is marketable. no owner can afford to be careless about their possessions. fox thoughts. that the "rational" and "reasonable" route advocates merely for less destructive and more profitable forms of exploitation. when we speak about "unnecessary" cruelty we imply both that some cruelty *is* necessary, and that "fair" treatment inside of a system enacting that cruelty would be an acceptable compromise. i don't believe there *are* any good forms of the animal industrial complex, and as a poor person, i don't want tolerable working conditions, i *want* the abolition of work. taking a life – *using up* a life – isn't wrong or tragic because of the "value" that life might have otherwise brought to the world, but because it *is* a life, singular and entire.

+

fox pelvis, like a three-dimensional rorschach. dog sniffs at it, unsteadily circles it, slopes away. he too is getting old. i read an article in which the ageing female author reflects that her dead body is now undoubtedly worth more than her live one. in america, she tells us, a disarticulated cadaver, broken down into about sixty different tissues, its component parts processed and made into medical products, is worth up to $250,000 on the open market. value production turns everything from body parts to crude oil to this book into commodity. when i picture it, it is as a great conveyor belt encircling the world. like Jörmungandr, the Midgard Serpent, only more banal thus more terrible. the morning is grim and i should be working, but the pressure to produce stifles my ability to do so. in my worst moments i see my intellectual labour as just another product in this conveyor belt economy. at cambridge, my friend sends me a poem, both for my "research" and to "spur" me on. the poem is 'The Thought Fox' by Ted Hughes. hum. i don't know how to feel about that. i like those moments in the penultimate and final stanzas, the fox 'coming about its own business', entering 'the dark hole of the head', which are so eloquent about the way animals inhabit and obsess us. but i'm uneasy about the fox: reduced to metaphoric freight, a figure for writing itself, or the mental processes *of* the writer. i don't like that Hughes in particular, as both hunter and self-mythologising poet, lays claim to fox qualities, fox affinities. in interviews down the years the impetus for 'The Thought Fox' is retold and refashioned, but each version involves the reproving intervention of a dream fox figure, appearing before Hughes the struggling cambridge undergraduate as he wrestles with an essay. in an early incarnation of this story, the essay was on Dr Johnson, and the fox shook his head wearily at the unfinished pages, which burst into flames. the next day Hughes wrote a poem, of which his nightly visitor more assuredly approved. in another variation, the fox was a therianthropic Hughes, with large vulpine head. in another, a burning man-fox 'stepped out of a furnace', blistered and burnt and in horrible pain. it presses a bloody paw to the pages of Hughes' essay and tells him to 'stop this – you are destroying us.' it's a good story. but i'm not wild about that 'us'. what could the stifled creativity of one cambridge under-graduate mean to a suffering beast? Hughes' story incorporates the devastating pain of an animal other into a self-dramatising gesture, one that suggests an equivalence between the manifest agony of the abject animal, and the mental anguish of a struggling student. why should the fox – in all of its uncanny singularity – be interested in Hughes at all? as if the writer's preoccupation with their chosen animal totem were a two-way street. for Hughes, hunting and fishing constituted a kind of enhanced participation in the natural world. in his best writing you sometimes feel him struggling to square this with the sense of desecration that follows the violent death of the animal. basically, it's weird to me that the fox asked Hughes to 'stop' writing essays, not killing foxes.

+

Hughes isn't unique. literary imagination freights the fox more than perhaps any other animal. in the west, Aristotle came first, framing her as a sinister trickster, formed from gristle and bone. all animals classified as inferior or "cold and earthy" were similarly constituted, but fox was singled out for particular disapprobation as being the polar opposite of man, furthest away of all the beasts from god. her dwelling in burrows only heightened her association with the underworld. but even further back there is the myth of the malevolent Teumessian Fox, an outsized vulpine monster that struck fear into the heart of thebes, and was destined, moreover, never to be caught. the *physiologus* ran with the image of the fox as both cunning and malign. this, from the cambridge university library bestiary:

> vulpis the fox gets his name from the person who winds wool (volupis) – for he is a creature with circuitous pug marks who never runs straight but goes on his way with tortuous windings.

> he is a fraudulent and ingenious animal. when he is hungry and nothing turns up for him to devour, he rolls himself in red mud so that he looks as if he were stained with blood. then he throws himself on the ground and holds his breath, so that he positively does not seem to breathe. the birds, seeing that he is not breathing, and that he looks as if he were covered in blood with his tongue hanging out, think he is dead and come down to sit on him. well, thus he grabs them and gobbles them up.

> the devil has the nature of this same.

for the purpose of most european bestiary texts, the fox is allegorised as the devil, who pretends to be dead to those not fully committed to christ, revealing his true nature only when the ensnared sinner is past all help. but the fox has other manifestations, more ambivalent than strictly devilish. for example, medieval literature's most famous vulpine antagonist: Reynard the Fox. he comes in many guises: as an iconoclast, as a corrupt killer, as a rapist and adulterer, lastly as a heroic underdog. his legend is slippery, hiding itself throughout the enlightenment within children's literature, performing fox-feats of slyness and concealment as his story crosses from dutch to english, morphs from adult satire to nursery fable. yet, all the while Reynard preserves something of his fundamental self. he is a trickster archetype (Lévi-Strauss, 1963): one who subverts moral and social expectations, traversing and transgressing the social order by bringing disorder, or creating order out of foolishness or deception.

+

Reynard stories were a popular staple of the allegorical folk tale across europe from the twelfth century onwards. at ely cathedral's stained glass museum, there are two foxy roundels that may or may not represent Reynard: one from the 15th century of a fox in a pulpit, upright in clerical get up "preaching" to geese, and another from the 18th century of a somewhat less anthropomorphic fox, stealing a goose or duck. Reynard has persisted and his representations across literary and visual culture are various. the most well-known version of the Reynard tales is the *romance of reynard the fox*, and it's quite something: while on the surface, these stories appear as bawdy or comic adventures, they are also marked by a satirical tone aimed pointedly at medieval society's most cherished institutions, particularly within later versions of the tales, where Reynard is used to take pot-shots at the aristocracy and to criticise both political and ecclesiastical corruption. although Reynard is presented as devious, amoral, cowardly and self-seeking, his readers also root for him; his cunning and ruthlessness are presented as necessities for survival. he represents a triumph of craft and mental agility over brute strength and social power, attributes typically personified by Brun, the gluttonous bear, and by Reynard's arch nemesis, the greedy and dull-witted wolf, Isengrim. perhaps the beast tale is able to broach criticism of the social order precisely because its protagonists occupy outsider status. in the case of Reynard, by voicing dissent through a morally dubious non-human instrument, the authors conceal their own intent and sympathies, addressing, so to speak, two audiences at once. so far so foxy, but perhaps it is more complex and more disturbing than that: to what extent were Reynard's first readers intended to identify with the foxy figure and his feral hustle? or, for that matter, with *any* of the tale's animal *types*. what is the relationship between the literary denigration of the animal, and its violent physical denigration in the world? lest we forget, it was only after the wolf was exterminated from most of europe that a concerted effort began to destroy the fox. or bear-gardens, they were a popular pastime in the middle-ages, chained animals mauled by dogs, or whipped and muzzled, forced to perform "tricks" for human spectators. even in their extremis, were these animals ever considered to be real, fully alive, feeling entities? or were they as much a figure for something else as their textual counterparts? this thought lodges painfully at the back of my brain. what does it mean to convert an animal life into a mere representation of its spectator's humanity? poor people saw a metaphor for their own suffering in the fate of the bears, but that's not to say they cared about them. who is to know? is this what we call "sympathy" or "solidarity" with the animal other? or is seeing ourselves in them a way of reducing the animal to a flat ideological cipher? if so, is Reynard different?

+

maybe. maybe, because the fox is different. it asserts its autonomy, refuses to work in accordance with human desire (Berger, 1980). the fox looks back. the fox refuses to be corralled, controlled, administered, reduced: exterminated like the wolf, territorialised like the bear. the fox looks weak and small compared with these larger animals, but his intelligence and daring have assured his survival. this is as true in real-life as it is Reynard's romances. the wolf was effectively obliterated from europe not only because it was hunted – persecuted – out of existence, but because its habitat was destroyed. the wolf could not adapt to survive in the new landscapes created by human encroachment. foxes, on the other hand, are superbly flexible synanthropic and commensal animals (O'Connor, 2013). again, a synanthropic species is one whose adaptation and development has been driven by the pressure of close cohabitation with humans. synanthropes play environments and logics hostile to their very existence back against themselves in order to thrive. so too with language. a 'renardie' that exaggerates and trumps the eloquence weaponised by the powerful. Reynard's very life depended upon adaptation and disguise, and in the tales that surround him, his mercurial nature is reflected in his mode of speech, characterised by wit and whip-quick linguistic dexterity. medieval scholar Jean Scheidegger coined the term 'renardie' or 'foxiness' for the coruscating verbal art in *the romance of reynard the fox.* for Scheidegger, 'renardie' reverses power relationships by flipping assumptions about relative degrees of agency and dynamism, demonstrating simultaneously the 'lawlessness of writing and its ability to set its own laws' (1989). given that a lack of verbal competence has been used to deny variously personhood, agency, and rights to both human and non-human others alike, Reynard's rhetorical virtuosity is significant. linguistic competence – and later print competence – has enormous power to summon an imagined community among

84

lettered elites, excluding those verbally stunted subjects who cannot properly be said to belong. it is not only that the written word transmits specific instances of legal and moral authority, but that both authority and status are implicit within the act of writing itself. *eloquence* is power, becomes a political tool to wield against stuttering, stammering, or silently oppressed bodies. Reynard subverts that power in a really interesting way: not only does his supple use of language go so gleefully against the grain of established hierarchies, but his performative parries privilege fleeting improvisation over the lumbering, top-heavy manoeuvres of his social betters. their linguistic power has become swollen and stiff through dint of complacent habit. Reynard, with a kind of pressurised vigour, wields a living language as sword and shield. this isn't the fox as a figure for language, this is language performing the fox, revelling in the escapologist potentials of both.

+

this morning a live fox. his narrow back canted away from me, sprinting. the dog scents his musk long after he's gone: orris-pungent, all meaty scat and tangy pheromone. joy. dead fox at the furrow. but fox will go on. yalla yorlins flitting round her bones. my head is *full* of fox thoughts. i get a lift to work. we drive past a pub called – not very imaginatively – the fox and hounds. signage bears the likeness of a fox in hacking jacket and jodhpurs. it is idiotic, but this kind of iconography serves a purpose. as if the fox were a willing participant in an equal contest. the repetition of such representations works to exaggerate the fox's cunning so as not to acknowledge her vulnerability. screwy logic that seeks to justify the hunt by two mutually exclusive arguments; that must see the fox as abject and inferior while simultaneously framing her as a worthy adversary. hunter logic: foxes hunt and so do we, therefore we are the same, morally equivalent. that's sympathy-retardant tory logic. *tóraidhe*, from the irish for *pursuer*. and aren't we all, pursued? still. there's something else in that image. transhuman "passing," hiding in plain sight. you have a sport, *tóraidhe,* you bally-hoo looser, you. fox has a game.

+

game, noun: an activity that one engages in for amusement or fun. / *game*, noun: a form of competitive activity or sport played according to rules. / *game*, noun: a secret and clever plan or trick. / *game*, noun: wild animals or birds hunted for food or sport. / *game*, noun: the flesh of wild animals or birds used for food. / *game*, adjective: willing to try something new or challenging. / *game*, verb: to manipulate a situation in a way that is unscrupulous or unfair.

+

the fox is *game*. is ludic and riddling. fox is risk and ominous jest. is insomnia's scavenging avatar. fox lurks, cheats, tricks, haunts. in cambridge there are rich pickings. walking home from a reading, there's a fox among the wheelie bins, along the backs, looping itself through the flaking railings. one of my students tells me that a fox craps on the lawn at king's college. when i look at the fox i see myself small in her eyes. she blinks, i disappear. her sauntering trespass is beautiful. i want to *be* fox, how i wanted to be dog as a child. or, i want to find a way of *being* fox, doing fox. i have reached once more the limits of my language, my capacity to be or do *human*. i am tired. i am in pain. i think of Simone Weil, how she writes that pain itself, 'is a pure quality, a state of mind which does not belong to any location'. there is 'no space in pain', she says, 'our pain, as a thought, extends throughout the world (if one looks at a fine landscape when one is in terrible pain one cannot admire it). the pain fills our whole universe.' (2015). like Coleridge, in 'Dejection: An Ode', staring blankly into the west, trying to wrest some scrap of spiritual consolation from indifferent nature, knowing full-well the futility of such an endeavour. i fold in on myself in the street. deep breaths, keep moving. you cannot quite accept pain, as Weil later advocates, because pain is not yours to accept *or* reject. there is no choice, so there can be no negotiation, pain simply is. this pain. i roll the words *umwelt* and *weltschmerz* round and around in mind and mouth. i had been talking to my student about pain and its inescapable circuit. they are a fine poet. they write of themselves in chronic pain as an animal. i think of Deleuze: 'the man who suffers is a beast, the beast who suffers is a man' (1996). which has nothing to do with "descent" to some degraded state on the part of man, or spiritual ascent through purifying agony on the part of the animal, the two somehow meeting in the middle. it has to do – amongst other things – with how the animal inhabits time. their relationship to reality and duration, surely so different to our own. not necessarily that animals are pure presence, locked in their present, dominated by their urges, but that in suffering, both humans and non-humans enter a state of time – like carceral time – in which the body is the only calendar, the only clock. we are incarcerated by and in pain. pain does indeed fill our whole universe, temporally as much as spatially. for human beings, language is a huge part of how we enter and measure time, it is relational and made. *artificial.* pain closes the gap between animal and man, we can no longer forget that we are bodies, that our experience of the world is mediated through or governed by our bodies. pain is not abstract. it is only in the moment that i apprehend the singular vulnerability of my own body in the world, that the bodies of suffering others come vividly into focus. we inhabit the unbearable, overwhelming "now" of pain, not together, but in common. my student is an animal. *feral.* maybe pain has its uses? i think of Audre Lorde's *cancer journals,* where the suffering body becomes a spur to solidarity with others who suffer (1980). the animal and i are not the same, that's not the point, but we *meet* in pain, i recognise their particularity and difference, their *self*. sometimes i think we spend our lives asleep, anaesthetised to those suffering selves, so that we can pass our days without the disgust or immobilising distress caused by the evidence of their destruction. i believe – i *know* – that killing animals for meat is a vile act, but i don't stand in the supermarket weeping. we say "roadkill" when we pass pheasants, badgers, rabbits, foxes en route to work, but the sight of them doesn't make or break my day. *i see you*, i whisper to the fox. she is unimpressed by my mental contortions. disappears between discarded scooters, cardboard crates, a spilled carton of wonton noodle soup. we forget, i suppose. most of us, for whom pain is a disruption to the homogenous structure of experience, something bright and fleeting. we remember *that* we were in pain, we don't remember *being* in pain, and that is the difference. chronic or constant pain is *different*. it creates a zone of sustained and radically sensitised attention to the experience of the body. and by extension the bodies of other others. i see you, fox. and i cannot be or do you, the animal is not something i can escape into. you experience pain every bit as acute and enduring as my own. i can only honour that pain, alongside the special gestures and forms of grace that fox bodies make possible at the margins of the "human" world.

+

Ted Hughes thought he had problems. god. he might have abandoned Dr Johnson or the english tripos or whatever it was he claimed to be wrestling with, but he stayed at and graduated from cambridge, for all his burning foxes. i will stay too, although my tenure will be far shorter. despite my wailing and gnashing of teeth, despite my hatred of privilege, and my immense loneliness, on my good days i am still less interested in rehashing the myth of some struggling creative stifled by hostile academia than i am in finding ways to productively undo the classist logics that govern the university. any university. i don't fool myself into believing that my mere presence is enough. i don't like the narrative that exceptionalises working-class individuals at the expense of their class cohorts. i am neither a symbolic victory nor a representational triumph. i am not an apologist for my "tribe" – whoever they are – or emblematic somehow of *all* working-class others, inside the academy or out. this model of inclusion is bullshit, it has been used to selectively edit notions of working-class identity within cultural space. through a persistent and myopic focus on one or two big name ambassadors, elites control the versions of ourselves permitted to proliferate and thrive. for example, post-war-northern-male as one of the few acceptable faces of working-class identity that has been allowed to flourish within contemporary poetry. that's deliberate: the poetry's distance from the material realities it describes presupposes and encodes a nostalgia, a looking back that defuses potential threat – social or poetic – and softens the language of experience. further, it contributes to the idea that the class system itself no longer exists by tying it to defunct forms of industrial labour, and the outdated social roles this labour engendered. this removes the experience of class-based oppression from black and brown others, especially women, especially queers, and especially those working within the increasingly exploitative service economy.

+

it's getting better. but those holding the purse strings still have nothing to gain from supporting projects that challenge or threaten their traditional business model; they're wary of a working-class poetics that openly and explicitly acknowledges the politics of its own oppression. to secure the invaluable financial assistance by which creative projects live or die, is – in some sense – to accept that your work, and that you, as a person, will be mediated, filtered and enmeshed by and in the machinery of hierarchy. through this process we are compromised: we tailor and shape our voices to fit their image of us, and our class identity is depoliticised through an act of effortful caricature. this is an old tune. a stuck record. i bore myself with my banging on, but i'm struggling with what it means to be here, to have applied for this position, to have taken this money. what did i want, and how did i think it would be? in the library, i read a review of my predecessor's work. it is spiteful. and it involves a shifty little manoeuvre that claims othered subjects lose the right to express the politics of their oppression at the exact moment they are granted the ability to be heard. she's here, so she's mid-dle-class. what *is* that? it happens all the time, particularly to those articulating class-based grievances. the thesis is that you, personally, have "transcended" your poor and working-class roots; that you, personally, are "no longer" working-class, and any claim to the contrary is a fraudulent play for pity-points or cultural kudos. *you've* got a position, *you've* made money, so *you've* no right to speak. but why *are* ambitious, successful, employed, and working-class mutually exclusive things to be? whose vision of the working-class is that? and where are you drawing the line, where's your threshold, how much do you have to be earning before the alchemy of transformation takes place? does it matter what kind of job? am i more completely transfigured than the roofer or the plumber who earns so much more than me? is it my wages, or my savings? is it something as intangible as my "social mobility"? what do you understand by that term? do you assume that taking up space is the same as being accepted, included, wanted, at ease? my friends and i joke that *i'm* "sooo middle-class now" because i go to conferences, and eat bougie avocado on toast (not even sorry), but our laughter turns as much on the shallowness of those tropes as my imperfect embodiment of them. i can eat all the smashed avocado i want (and i will) but i'm still just some pleb stuffing a fancy sandwich in her face. animal in people clothes. my disguise is fooling no one, least of all myself. the idea that being here magically remakes me as a clean, sleek, aspirational version of myself is fucking insulting on a number of levels. firstly, it misunderstands what poverty is, what it can do to people. poverty is traumatic, is trauma. which inscribes a perpetual present, which has no – can have no – expiriation date. yet people do this all the time, apply a statute of limitations to the wound of raw experience, demand a narrative trajectory of healing and recovery in line with the normalising aspirations of neo-liberal culture. and if this is a logic applied to the shocking and readily legible wound, then of course we must meet it in the invisible realm of economic violence. that's *not* how trauma works, though. traces will remain with you forever, the behaviours and strategies you learnt to survive while in extremis will shape and contour your experience of the world for the rest of your life. if you have kids, you'll pass it down to them with varying degrees of consciousness. you will never shake the fear, the absolute debil-itating rage, the insecurity of not being safe, or "good enough", of never being listened to, of being rejected, spoken over, spoken down to, spoken about, administered, shunted, shuffled to the back. poverty is not only a set of material circumstances (although it is, first and foremost, definitely that) that one can "overcome" or "leave behind". you don't lose the right to talk about that or to advocate for your class cohort because by some miracle you've improved your economic, educational, or cultural opportunities. to pivot, poverty is also inseparable from the *joy* of cohort, family, and culture. it's the texture of your pleasures, your insights, your sense of style. why should you want or expect to let that go? it's the rangy scope of your thoughts, it's the extent and limit of their expression; it is your use of language. "you're middle-class now" claims that you were nothing before you were here, that you've jettisoned your past and its affects, or that you no longer have the moral right to access them. bollocks. and it's not about mining our experiences in order to write, but that those experiences have shaped the *way* we write. as my body bears the scars and traces of classed experience, so too does my mind. what is best in my practise, that which is valued by the publications and institutions employing me, is precisely that which pertains to poverty and to class. i can't relax here. i don't know how.

+

the irish poet, Patrick Kavanaugh used to attend fancy shindigs in dublin with clods of cow-shit on his boots. the cow-shit was a deliberate affront to a literary culture that wanted the myth and the fruits of rural irish labour without its material traces. the shite was literal evidence of this labour, but it was also a figure for how cultural elites treat all such evidence of classed identity. it was a stumbling block to self-congratulation amongst those who discovered, feted and "rescued" the poet, as if that were something he needed or wanted. it was also a pungent aide-mémoire for Kavanaugh himself, a remonstrance against denial or forget-fulness. not in some half-baked rose-tinted way. the opposite, in fact, for if your roots are quite literally in shit, then it is very difficult to affect sentimentality about the dear ol' homestead. shite is an injunction to remember without romanticising the past. there is struggle in it. it is impossible to ignore. it adheres to you, you carry and track it in. it offends, it embarrasses, it is of the animal, of the body.

+

i am watching a Q&A with the black american poet, Patricia Smith. her poetry a form of incendiary activism inside lyric imagination. questions from the floor, and somebody asks her if sometimes she wouldn't like to write about flowers. wow. an implied "instead" hangs over the hall. Smith points out that as a black woman writing inside of english in america she is an inescapably politicised presence. to write about flowers would be, for her, a political act, whether she willed it or not. in an email my friend says she admires the way i convert sorrow into ambition. but what's to admire? sometimes i am afraid. perhaps we have learnt to *convert* sorrow into ambition, art, whatever, because we know that our sorrow, pure sorrow has no validity here, no traction, will never be countenanced. this too is political.

+

my body wears down according to its classed and economic history. inequality of access and provision are written into my terrible teeth, my nails, my skin, my squint, my aching back, my untreated pain. i am Kavanaugh's cow-shit. i cling to myself. a colleague talks to me about "burn-out" and all i can see is a caravan in flames, a treeline on fire. i think about burning the forest to smoke out the fox. i think of Hughes 'burnt fox'. i think about traveller families burnt out of their homes, animalised as vermin, invasive and encroaching. i think about catholic families, evicted by arson in belfast during the sixties. i think about how, during the reformation, protestant propaganda depicted foxes as duplicitous catholics – up to and including the Pope! unusual for fox representations, the Lutheran fox-Pope tricks from a position of power: arch-hypocrite, he pretends to the meek and peaceful sleep of the lamb. wake him to discover his 'fox-craft'. witches were foxes. witches too were burnt. women became foxes to frustrate the hunt. women became foxes to evade capture

by their own pursuers. everything hurts and everything burns.
"i mean you look tired". oh.

+

i carry the fox with me into my working day, and i find myself
thinking of Moten and Harney, writing in *the undercommons:
fugitive planning & black study* (2013). they say:

> the only possible relationship to the university today
> is a criminal one
>
> "to the university i'll steal, and there i'll steal," to borrow
> from pistol at the end of henry v, as he would surely
> borrow from us. this is the only possible relationship
> to the american university today. this may be true of
> universities everywhere. it may have to be true of the
> university in general. but certainly, this much is true in
> the united states: it cannot be denied that the university
> is a place of refuge, and it cannot be accepted that the
> university is a place of enlightenment. in the face of
> these conditions one can only sneak into the univer-
> sity and steal what one can. to abuse its hospitality, to
> spite its mission, to join its refugee colony, its gypsy
> encampment, to be in but not of—this is the path of
> the subversive intellectual in the modern university.
>
> [...]
>
> but for the subversive intellectual, all of this goes on
> upstairs, in polite company, among the rational men.
> after all, the subversive intellectual came under false
> pretenses, with bad documents, out of love. her labor
> is as necessary as it is unwelcome. the university needs

what she bears but cannot bear what she brings. and
on top of all that, she disappears. she disappears into
the underground, the downlow lowdown maroon
community of the university, into the undercommons
of enlightenment, where the work gets done, where
the work gets subverted, where the revolution is still
black, still strong.

these words galvanise me. these words promise both a way of
being in the space of the university, and way of *doing* thought.
for all our difficult bodies. these words *feel* foxy. and i wonder
if we can walk with fox these circuitous and winding paths to
social sabotage, deviancy, sedition? can we squat the storied social
structures of the *english* university, with claggy scoot, insouciant
strut? fox becomes posterchild for the margins: a bandit, a rebel,
a russet upsetter, citizen of the undercommons. this is absolutely
about how we take up space, how we repurpose the university's
neglected corners through physical occupation, but this is also a
mode of thinking and writing against the disciplinary correctness
of the academy, the expectations of tutors and colleagues. it is
a lively and promiscuous relationship to discourse. it embraces
Halberstam's notion of 'low theory'. that is, insufficiently or eccentrically theorised, bristling with strange rigour. not professional,
not productive, a bug in the system of 'reduction and demand'.
fox-craft. and proud. fox will indeed 'sneak into the university and
steal' what she can. fox is a feral manifesto made fur, a refusal of
the binary prescription upon which the entire neoliberal project
is founded, where worthy knowledge and culture are extracted,
and the dross is discarded as criminality or waste. fox lives and
thrives amid the discards. exults and excels in the criminal and
quasi-legal. on the dung heap. in the skip. rummaging among the
refuse. we too are assumed to be here under 'false pretences', by
underhanded trickery. our practice becomes to practice against.

what does it mean to lean into that? grifters, gaming the rubes.

+

fox, wiping its arse on the manicured lawn. fox is scummy. fox
dirt is a kind of culture jam. is culture nixed. hexed. her very persistence in this highfalutin world functions as a form of *unwork*
or fuck-up. as Valerie Solanas writes in the *SCUM manifesto*:

> SCUM will keep on destroying, looting, fucking-up
> and killing until the money-work system no longer
> exists [...] until enough women cooperate with SCUM
> to make violence unnecessary to achieve these goals,
> that is, until enough women either unwork or leave
> work, start looting, leave men, and refuse to obey all
> laws inappropriate to a truly civilised society.

while established feminist movements urged dissatisfied house-
wives to seek gainful employment beyond the home as an avenue
to freedom and self-fulfilment, Solanas advocated for something
entirely different: identifying capitalism itself as the fulcrum of
women's exploitation, she demanded a perpetual labour shutdown
in which women would appear to accept jobs only to do bad work,
break rules and equipment, get fired, and repeat ad infinitum,
until the entire apparatus collapsed. devious. devilish. *foxy.* but
also reminiscent of those higher forms of stupidity evoked by our
old friend the chess playing chicken. this is *playing* dumb, as the
fox in the bestiary plays dead, as a snare to the unwary. to enter
the academy you've got to be game. "play the game." join the game
in order to cheat, to forfeit, to vandalise and obstruct. surpass,
outclass. or else contrive a fail so epic it involves all other players.
foxiness cultivates underestimation, of both your competence
and your resistive potential. we can learn from fox. and we can
learn as much from all that has been interpolated onto her; from

the way she conceals her true self inside these myriad cultural projections. for all our words, she remains unmoved. she remains free. fox lives to fight another day. and so will we. and so will i.

COMMUNITY & HAUNTING /
THE HAUNTED COMMUNITY

what the writing *wants*, what my *feral* is trying to do: to summon a community; to confront that which makes community impossible. he says community is *not* impossible. he says i *need* a community. he thinks i have been seduced by the myth of the rugged outsider, that i'm one step away from Rosemary Tonks. or Ted Kaczynski. but he's wrong. or he misunderstands me. what i mean is that *human* community can never be experienced, cannot even be imagined, can only be mourned. the only time such a community comes into focus, the only time we can truly apprehend *ourselves*, is when we are made malignantly visible by tragedy. i will sing you the ballad of the bonny portmore and explain to you that colonised peoples already live inside your aftermath. the collapse you fear has already engulfed us. *this* is the epilogue to a vast environmental devastation. that song, so you know, dates back to the 1700s and the felling of ireland's oldest oak forest, of which the Great Oak of Portmore was metonymic and symbolic. in our earliest alphabet (ogham) the letters corresponded to trees. out of the 16,000 town-lands in ireland, 13,000 are named after trees (derry and kildare are called after *dair*, or *oak*, and killarney literally means *church of the blackthorn*). from the 8th century ireland had an entire law corpus (brehon law) regarding the preservation and stewardship of trees, to the extent that they were awarded legal considerability, treated as living and in some instances *sacred* beings. after the "planters" did their work, destroyed the forests, they left not only a landscape irreparably changed, but a set of legal and cultural relationships to and with the natural world – to everything in short that signifies *home* – utterly smashed. that song is a haunting, it summons as it mourns the oak, the community.

+

community is made in the sweating palms of absolute loss, hands that know to reach and not to hold. the community is a hand born hungry, is an aftermath, a hindsight. we coalesce around the weary fact of our shattering. we are only aware of the lung when we struggle to breathe. before the disaster – whatever disaster – we were merely selves. but they look at us differently now. two's company, catastrophe's a crowd. a chorus. i might *want* a community, but our time is now, and our time is never, always emergent, forever delayed, an impossible commons, a commons of impossible bodies. community requires a past, desires a future. you *need* a community, he says, but i carry its cancelled weight in the dross of all my doings.

+

not seduced. the "lone wolf" is not a myth, but she *is* an outlier. wolf packs create their pariahs too. hierarchy is socially useful to animals other than humans. and i'm not some lunatic prepper. i know that individual freedom requires social support. to make meaningful choices, you need others to respect and support that choice. to exercise freedom of movement, you need others to facilitate this movement, not to erect walls, turnstiles, chain-link, checkpoints, borders, and roadblocks. for change to be effected, others must endorse – at least accept – that change. freedom is a social relationship, and our freedoms are mutually dependent. you *can't* invoke the free individual without evoking the spectre of community. the two are inseparable. but if freedom is a social relationship – better, a *set* of social relationships – what happens when you subject those relationships to intolerable pressure? through assimilation and dispersal? through gentrifi-cation? through violence? community requires a place, a space of recognition and release where it is possible to make our way back to ourselves through each other. break up the sites, tear down the squats, "clean up" our neighbourhoods. the impossibility of community is not perhaps a question of marginality, not anymore. the margins *were* our dwelling place, our gathering ground: to dance, to laugh, to grieve, and to create. the horror of assimilation is that it cannot tolerate a margin. the goal is your forcible incorporation inside a system that despises you. let's say that community is the organisation of social relationships, guided by a shared set of underlying principles towards some kind of specified end (an artist's co-op, an allotment, a more sustainable existence within nature, whatever). organisation is the expression of hope, the possibility of change; it requires a future we can imagine ourselves into. it needs the idea of an elsewhere, an otherwise. assimilation is inescapable. or naturalised as so absolutely inevitable as to trap us in an endlessly expanding and repeating present. in which – again – we have no stake. these are also the broader logics of catastrophe capitalism, with its narrative of common and sinister doom. if we are told that the future – any future – is quite literarily impossible, how will we find the imaginative strength to agitate for *alternative* futures? how can we project ourselves forward, propose change, broach meaningful challenge? it isn't merely that we become habituated to disaster; that we lose the horror and the pity of it to apathy and helplessness. it isn't even that the crisis is so all-encompassing as to render our individual efforts futile. it is, rather, that the idea of ecological collapse is so amorphous and so vast as to obscure its own highly specific, local, and eminently resistible causes. to say nothing of those responsible. it is not, in fact, some kind of all-consuming great leveller. we will all be touched *by* climate violence and environmental collapse, but we are not all equally to blame. nor will we all be equally affected.

+

to live inside the aftermath is to foreclose even the imaginative possibility of a future, isn't it? or can an aftermath be an ethics too? having lived *through* can we translate our faltering expressions of care into new forms of social relation? for instance, the suspension of property. how after M died every door on the street stood open, the women went from house to house, the children fed from whoever's kitchen. as if there'd been an earthquake, a landslide, a fire. how you live when you're standing in the rubble of your lives. the structures of rescue and relief are necessary, but aren't they as much about reclaiming these nascent communities as anything else? absorbing them back into the structural limits of the state? half the world burns, the other half drowns. i've been thinking about this a lot lately. somebody says "sustainability". i mentally strip the word back to its sticky, disavowed *stain*: to endure, to withstand, to tolerate and perpetuate, to have inflicted upon and to suffer that infliction. environmental damage, human misery. what exactly is it we are being asked to preserve? what exactly is it we are being asked to withstand? isn't this a word, after all, for the sickly regimes of capitalist accumulation? i see you, growth-mindsetters, greenwashing the wound.

+

it is said that while people can imagine the end of the world, they cannot imagine an end to capitalism. what *feral* wants, what my poetry wants, is to bridge this imaginative void, where all our solutions and escapes must fall within the same market system, a system that exists in such painful and inherent antagonism to the care of the biotariat and to the dignity of life. poetry, thriving on leaps of logic, associative connections, and visceral imagery, offers us a way to vividly conceptualise our entanglement in this machinery. not to diagnose a problem – we are *way* beyond that – but to extend the possibility of radical change. i think what i mean by that is that poetry itself is my community, albeit a kind of ghost community; that community is what *haunts* my poetry, in terms of places and people long gone, but also in terms of its pure *idea*. inside the poem the care and control i exert is a care and control that is seldom afforded us as citizens or subjects. the poems that contain these expressions of care function as small units of resistance; they struggle to hold their shape against the distortional stresses of a difficult, unequally valued life. this is a work of militant cherishing that wants to inscribe a loved and perpetual present, a space for us, somewhere 'between the actual and the possible' (Marx, 1897); against cold, against grot, against alienation and unemployment in all its reductive brutality, against the animal industrial complex, violent waste, toxic spew, the poem wants to erect an alternative dialectical tenderness. the poem, our only possible place.

+

how does *ghost* relate to *feral?* first through the uncanny experience of being forced to grieve in the future-conditional for catastrophic and unprecedented species loss. second, through the notion of 'hauntology' as coined by Jacques Derrida in *spectres of marx* (1993). while Derrida's specific claim is about the atemporal nature of Marxism and its tendency to 'haunt western society from beyond the grave', the term as it is used today typically refers to the return or strange persistence of a variety of elements from the social or cultural past, as in the manner of a ghost. does an extinct animal continue to exercise a powerful pull on our collective imagination; what does it mean to engage with these cultural and representational traces? or with the material afterburns of violent dispossession: these impacts, indents, remainders, stains? on a fraught visit to family, i am pursued around a strange city by dodo graffiti, bearing the legend: 'si estingue solo chi rifiuta di volare'. what does that mean? it means 'only those who refuse to fly are extinguished'. i have never seen a dodo, not even a sawdust filled specimen. i know little about the bird apart from the fact of its extinction. the dodo has become metonymic for extinction, an untenanted bird-shaped sign that no longer stands for itself. i detest that 'refusal to fly' logic, it's so much social darwinism. but i also hate more generally how the animal is flattened, out of shape, substance and grievability. there are a million kitschy cartoon dodos; its vivid and various after-life obscures the historical violence of extinction. i say to my niece that i think the desire to metaphorise the animal at all must be a kind of violence. she says: 'you can over think these things'. in the museum i touch the bones, i fog the glass inside of which stuffed birds tilt at unnatural angles. i think about the Hitchcock film, *psycho* (1960), where Norman Bates is confiding that he likes to practice taxidermy, mainly on birds, because 'birds look well stuffed' being only kind of 'passive' when alive. there's an extent to which we all perform the role of Norman Bates: nature frozen inside its cultural representations, as some kind of stuck, stuffed, material receptacle. even with the best of intentions: "preserve", "conserve", balance, replenish, maintain. as genetic repository or museum exhibit. static, without the potential to surge, intwine, expand, evolve. what comes into focus when i fog the glass, breathe on the bones? these dead are not here for their own sake, what they preserve is their niche in human knowledge, man's capacity to catalogue and map: genealogies, taxa. all those subtle histories, those movements of migration. for the animal we must look elsewhere.

+

and what about the city, this city or any other? the material wealth of the city is a slave-haunting, is a famine-haunting, is a murder-ghost. *you can over think these things.* topple the statues.

not for what they represent, but for who they erase, for the black, enslaved presence that can never occupy this city, only haunt it. the wealth of empire is made of meat. poor bodies do not create wealth, wealth is *made* of poor bodies, and poor black bodies in particular. we're not conditions of production, we're forms of fucking capital. worse, poor black bodies are *literally* wealth, a currency, the medium of exchange. something my friend K said to me: they don't live in this city, they *are* this city, subsumed into the fabric of its function. the rich live on through their monuments, architectural and cultural: buildings, statues, and street names all serve to capture the continuity of *their* lived experience, inscribing memory onto public space. canonical art and literature archive *their* histories, museums are full of *their* things. they stand for the past. they shore themselves up with it. *we* have few enduring possessions, and fewer opportunities to intervene in culture. we are excluded, therefore, from the long posterity these things engender. what they call *history* happens to us in interminable waves of force. my history, says K, begins with "a mark in a ledger", with the eerie numerals of market value. the city launders suffering like money. the poor circulate, cease to exist.

+

or, i am thinking of the absent animal, as a kind of 'negative evidence', where voids and elisions function as markers to annihilating violence. Eyal Weizman tells us that 'histories of violence will always have their lacunas and discontinuities. they are inherent in violence and trauma and to a certain extent evidence of them' (2017). for Weizman, the 'truth' of state violence is filtered through various photographic and informational 'thresholds' – territorial, juridical, and visual – which bring objects, persons and evidence in and out of visibility. omission. redaction. Weizman's work develops a 'forensic architecture' for the built environment, but does the *non*-human world demand a forensis too? an ecological reckoning that engages the negative space where the other should be? they name our estates after the trees our mildewed houses have replaced. these cherries, these birches, these larches, this ash. our presence here inscribes this loss: "it was a lovely area before you came", the money in my pocket is made from rendered tallow, it has been years since any of us heard the cuckoo. how do you measure such a loss? city kids who don't know the names of the animals. it's more than a wound in "biodiversity", but a way of being in the world. the garden is so silent. the deadening testimony of bees. soft tight bodies spent from pesticide.

+

here is Avery Gordon, writing in *ghostly matters* (1997):

> what's distinctive about haunting is that it is an animated state in which a repressed or unresolved social violence is making itself known, sometimes very directly, sometimes more obliquely. i used the term haunting to describe those singular yet repetitive instances when home becomes unfamiliar, when your bearings on the world lose direction, when the over-and-done-with comes alive, when what's been in your blind spot comes into view. haunting raises spectres, and it alters the experience of being in time, the way we separate the past, the present, and the future…

sit with that a minute.

+

trauma, which is also atemporal – even extra-temporal – lives on through its traces, through its aftermath, its effects of repetition and deferral. trauma-time is recursive and hiccupping, breaking in on the "present", is never not happening now. a ghost is the same: it fractures our traditional, linear conceptions of temporality. it is both "new"– born of moment, knocking aside its receiving subjects in a moment of shocked attention – and "from" the past, a dredging up and spinning out. a spitting out. bad words. blood and broken teeth.

+

hauntings are political. as politics itself is spectral: abusive power, oppressive yet subliminal, elided and denied. haunting is both a language for repressed social violence, and a model of experience. the ghost is that hidden thing becoming known to us. a ghost is a territory. a ghost is a calendar. those instances, says Avery Gordon, of 'singular yet repetitive' uncannying, a loss of bearings, a disruption to – and inside of – linear time and familiar place, collapsing the past and the present together. haunting is a temporal glitch. it is the impossible time of a love without object, expression or exit. *broken hearted i'll wander, broken hearted i'll remain.* trauma, which attaches to and penetrates the bodies, brains, and memories of those who experience it. yet also resistance. against, in the first place, the mandated amnesia of the state, whose practice of containment is so strenuous precisely because it is forever incomplete. a ghost is incommensurable. forgetting is effortful, exhausting. this compulsive need to memorialise the past is not about memory per se, but an attempt to erect a cordon sanitaire around the raw, recalcitrant grief of involuntary anamnesis. to bracket this pain within prescribed parameters: in the very instant the immaterial are materialised they are obliterated, forced back into canniness, the commensurable, mundane. *broken hearted i'll wander, broken hearted i'll remain.* and it's the wandering that scares them. broken heartedness is catching. when i return, which is not so often now, i am struck again by the way in which our ghosts are both consequence and cause. they are – *you* are, my love – a symptom of this violence, and a continued provocation to it. is a ghost, they ask, evidence or testimony? it is perhaps the eerie testimony that arises when evidence is rejected or missing. and ours are noisy ghosts, emissaries of an insolent, reckless, restless coming breed. poltergeists reflect not a dread of the future but its absolute refusal. that the past is here to stay or may erupt at any time from inside of the present. that the past is not only animate in the present, but capable of influencing and affecting it. not merely a *felt* thing. we are full of such survivals, and yes, we identify with them: we'll suck you through the television into the static, back and back. and of course we – the living – haunt ourselves. each other. we are figured as zombies, vampires, ghosts, boggarts, bogeys. because, where is the present we might safely and purposefully occupy? there is a void. a paralysis. *in your he-ad, in your he-e-ead…* oh lovely boy, in the tv the material violence of history and the spectral violence of the sign converge. and oh, body, you sweet calendar of conflict counting out the days. if you think there will be resolution, you can just forget it, pal.

+

when i write that politics is spectral, i mean that politics itself constitutes a way of disguising and transfiguring more overt forms of domination. fascism is the ghost that haunts both parliamentary democracy and neoliberal capitalism, etc. when i write that the feral subject lives out a kind of ghostly existence, i mean that the presence and possibility of death are tangible in marginalised and threatened lives, but also because we are rejected and vanished inside of culture, the product of superstitious fear, approached but never met, spoken around but seldom seen: absent subjects. it is and isn't this. i am haunted by haunting. i live in the wake of violence. that is, i travel in the slipstream and the shadow of its passage, in its quiver of disturbed flow. i am always coming *after.* i live in the wake of violence, that is, within its many traditions of vigil and merriment, the uncanny expectation of return. i live in the wake of violence, the crack of sparrows, the crock of an eye iced open with insomnia, the world asleep and violence and i, alone with our thoughts.

kitsch is the haunting violence makes in culture, our ancestors returned to us as dancing paper skeletons. in our video nasties the blood is too red to be real. it's not meant to be real. the blood is a kind of slapstick, the blood is a kind of slang, the blood exceeds and surpasses the blood. we do not find the blood comic or lacking in power, we find real blood less real. and it is. that is, real blood has both a literal and imaginative limit. maybe ten percent of the adult human body is blood. something like one point five gallons of it. the too-red blood is a reservoir, is a tidal wave, a tsunami. there is no end to the too-red blood: how much can be shed, how much we are expected to withstand. elevator doors go ping! and – o sluice, o cascade, o grand fucking rapids. the blood is a currency. it no longer has anything to do with the body or bodies that produced it. the blood is an event. the blood is the image exceeding the event. the blood is an ambiance. the blood is a figure of speech. the blood belongs to you, to all of us, to each of us. we are inside the blood now. cardboard belfast on the telly. i'm thinking about the day that bloke jumped from the flats on the cambridge, we stood behind the cordon. you were eating spicy doritos and you said: "it's raining men, hallelujah." i don't want people to get the wrong idea about you, it's not coldness that made you say that. we didn't see any blood. or, i'm thinking of that *life* magazine photo of Evelyn McHale, reproducing suicide as an angle of enigmatic repose. these shitlord art blogs banging on about the beauty of the image, and all i can think of is *how dare you!?!* and all i can think is that in the too-real world she would have been sliced and spurting. fetishise that!

you absolute fuckers! the blood is hysterical. is the maimed joke of the maimed. that's what schlock is.

+

schlock is feral. i want a poem that does what those films did. in which the suffering, diseased, necrotic body is rendered visible upon the space of the page. i want the dead and dying, so often cannibalised by the poem as lyric sustenance and transformed into bland, disembodied traces, to return to us full of pus and vomit, seeping, bloated, scabbed over, repulsive to look at and think about. see, poetry is involved in a process of mourning that simultaneously enshrines the dead in collective memory, while disguising the gruesome bodily facts of their dying, to say nothing of the historical and political context that forms the long biography of their suffering. culture now tends to frame both death and the traumatic loss engendered by death as unknow-able, "unspeakable", untouchable. yet, as Naomi Mandel notes, the well-worn concept of trauma as unrepresentable may well be a 'discursive production' that evades moral responsibility in representing atrocity by privileging the 'problems inherent in speech' rather than addressing the 'ethical obligations involved in such representations' (2006). a cop-out, in other words, and one expedient to the aims of power. how much is masked by propriety, by an aversion to the "gory" details?

+

did you know, the original grand guignol was named for the popular french puppet character, Guignol, whose first incarnation was as savvy social commentator, a spokesperson for beleaguered workers? well yes, that thing i just said. the working-class are a haunting too. i was thinking about bodies: the way in which western culture frequently figures society itself as a besieged organism, using this potent metaphor to conceptualise human and labour relations in merciless social-darwinist terms, while treating individual human bodies as blunt instruments, expendable resources, and faceless economic units. i was thinking about self-harm. i was thinking about the too-real blood as protest and performance: the amoral charades that render our waste and wasted bodies visible and potent. i was watching *child's play* and singing: "the people's flag is deepest red, it shrouded oft our martyred dead, and ere their limbs grew stiff and cold, their hearts' blood dyed in every fold…" and i was thinking about you. no offence.

+

it's that Chucky doll. *tiocfaidh ár lá* – rendered phonetically as 'chucky ar la' or 'our day will come'– is, as all good children know, the unofficial slogan of the irish republican army. it refers to the coming of a united and free ireland. in belfast, members of the irish republican army and its various splinter groups were colloquially referred to as 'chuckies'. the Chucky films are a late nineties horror-comedy franchise about a murderously malevolent doll of the same name: a cherubic, freckle-faced redhead, and a psychopathic killer. for some reason, Chucky's physical appearance embodies racist irish stereotypes up the fucking wazoo, imaginatively (albeit unintentionally) fusing irish identity and homicidal intent. something about the cartoon violence of the film speaks to the unreality, and to the limited, racially-inscribed understanding of civil war violence, for most people outside of ireland. it cracked us up. so i'm thinking about you, and i'm thinking about how much we loved those films, how the figure of Chucky became a kind of avatar. we borrowed him for a satire on the social, cultural, and political expectations that surrounded us: our own predisposition towards violence, our own revenant rage. haunted dolls, doubly unreal.

+

thinking about ghosts i tell my friend that i blame the cashless society, how it tricks people into believing that culture, and not economics, is the basis for political reality by making money invisible, ghostly. man, all this dicking around on the surface, armada of TERF!s, identarian wallowing. and she says, *didn't Althusser murder his wife?* and she says *what structural level?* maybe she has a point.

+

look, within the lyric, i am confronted yet again with the limits of merely feeling "sad". of droning on about my own pain in a psychopath-test falsetto. i'm not talking about your death at all, about any death. i can only write from the wake, in the wake, in the after woods. loss provokes this complex challenge to communication, comprehension, thought. here comes Adorno's often misunderstood assertion that to write poetry after auschwitz is either impossible, or barbaric (1949). but, as Mandel tells us, auschwitz became a word 'to refer to the limit of words, pointing toward a realm inaccessible to knowledge. speaking the unspeakable would extend or efface these limits, diminishing the distance between us and that realm [...] and forcing us to confront the implications of such effacement for thinking, writing, and speaking about what has been assumed to be unspeakable.' feral wants to circumvent or disrupt all the different conceptual and moral prohibitions on speech. the different registers of silence, shocked or coerced. will my non-human "speaker" *say* what a human speaker cannot? can feral borrow from "low-culture", from all those reviled or dismissed forms of cultural representation: the video nasty, the soap opera, the fanzine, the slapstick comedy? feral demands – and is – a form of speech written off as facile, banal, limited or dangerous. feral forms of culture are those consumed by the relatively powerless, they are what the powerless make from pain, not an escape from pain, nor pain's conversion, but an ethical and attentive witness to pain by other means.

+

segue: you can always tell a tory by the limited and sentimental nature of their compassion. they watch an advert about sad donkeys and they carry around a portable raincloud for a week. but they've still got their ipads, and they haven't cancelled their amazon subscriptions, and they still think we should be dumping our actual shit in the actual the sea, drilling a million actual holes in the earth's actual crust, letting desperate families drown in the actual channel. murder is overt, yet diffuse. i encourage you to remember the body, by throwing a bottle of boiling piss at these thugs asleep in their eiderdowns.

+

when i struggle to frame a thought, i slide into epistolarity, as if through an act of direct address i might call the dead back to presence. it is and it isn't the desire to animate – reanimate – the other of apostrophe. mine is an apostrophe of bad faith, serves only to foreground the absence of my addressees. it is a desperate gesture towards silence and the impossibility of reply. or, not reply, reception. it's not that they will not speak, it is that they cannot hear. the dead do not live here. the persons and communities i pour the work toward are gone. the epistolary is my own form of 'negative evidence'; i am pointing at the site of injury, at the wound left in listening by the violence of their death. ultimately, what haunts this writing is not presence-in-some-other-form, but absence. or it is writing *born* dead, and *for* the dead; its implied and intended cohort of readers are no longer here, are already gone, have *always* been gone. i give them the worst of my churning thoughts. who *else* could possibly receive them? where else do they belong? so these thoughts hang in the awkward silence of cancelled response. they breed irritation and discomfiture. the scene of writing is not "amongst friends", and the words that frame these thoughts can expect neither acceptance or reciprocity; they look for neither consolation or catharsis. i do not wish to engage in the polite work of memorialisation, to build the kind of lyric monument that replaces those people and places the poem purports to signify. any such attempt is, after all, doomed to failure. we can only hold the lost – whether people, places, objects – close by stopping their course. we trap them in amber, they lose their identities: stuffed. like nature under glass. the poem will not accept taxidermy as a substitute for life. it will not pretend the two are the same, or that "as-close-as-it-gets" is good enough. i want language to tell us about everything that language cannot solve. what loss does on the *level* of language, what it means to speak into the open space where our dead should be. again and again. i read this back to my brother. *man, that got dark quickly.* he buys me a notebook with a cartoon dinosaur on the front, speech bubble says: *all my friends are dead.* it's the kind of joke we're prone to. but how *would* it feel to be the last of something? live out your days in the negative time of extinction? which also makes you the first of something, singular, the only one of your "kind", creating yourself from yourself – like Raleigh's hyena – day after day, nothing to measure yourself against. what i mean when i say that community is impossible is that we are cancelled in both directions at once, and so the poem is what i do *instead* of community. the damaged joke, haunted by the *ghost* of laughter. a permanent possession. or, an endless "now" of bottomless potentiality.

+

or it is like this: Deleuze says that the difference between *tired* and *exhausted* is that 'the tired person has merely exhausted the realization, whereas the exhausted person exhausts the whole of the possible. the tired person can no longer realize, but the exhausted person can no longer possibilize' (1997). which is to say that in the weird liminal space of exhaustion, no one possibility is preferred or excluded over another according to any recognisable goal. rather, all possibilities coexist and are interchangeable. in exhaustion all possibilities exist in potentiality, without any kind of structure or plan. Deleuze's word is 'compossible'. the commons of the poem is such a space of anarchic potentiality: not something to be realised, but a contingency that can or cannot happen. it's a blank space, a non-preference, but it is also imminence, a place where the living and the dead converge. the poem is a kind of euphoric flourishing inside of exhaustion, where community *can* exist, with the non-human, the dead, with the light, with the weather, with the absent, with absence itself. just not *here,* in the world. only *here,* on the page, born on breath. the poem is always this reaching, its potential is never realised, so its work is never completed.

BEWARE OF THE BLOB /
SLIMER'S REVENGE

turning forty is listing to 'my friend goo' by Sonic Youth and thinking about *slime*. specifically, about an Irigarian metaphorics of slimy feminine alterity; Irigaray's injunction, in *an ethics of sexual difference*, to celebrate mucus for 'its abundance […] its availability, its joyousness, its flesh.' (1982). in the canons of classical aesthetics, the body is 'transcendental and monumental, closed, static, self-contained, symmetrical and sleek' (Russo, 2012). the ideal body, that rational envoy of high or official culture, that sovereign individual, is, somewhat predictably, male. the grotesque or abjected body is porous, slick – not sleek – absorbing and secreting; an irrational fuckscape of seeping ports, sucking holes. an orifice, a wound. female genitalia is wet, "slimy", is a challenge, according to Irigaray, to the solidity of male power as concentrated in and expressed through male bodies. more than this, *slime* gives the lie to an idea of the body as something solid and final. *slime* says *body* is not an object, but a process. better, a 'moment of organisation' in an expansive, open-ended process of connection that involves the corporeal, material, and symbolic realms. (Angel and Gibbs, 2017). this process of connection is myriad: fertilisation, the transfer of long protein strands through glowing mucous membranes, sex, infection, teeming bacteria, mycelial networks, death and decay. this thought really puts the wind up people.

+

for example, Sartre's discourse on slime in *being and nothingness* (1969). of handling slime he writes: 'i open my hands, i want to let go of the slimy, and it sticks to me, it draws me, it sucks at me. its mode of being is neither the reassuring inertia of the solid nor a dynamism like that in water which is exhausted in fleeing from me. it is a soft, yielding action, a moist and feminine sucking.' repeat: a *'moist and feminine sucking'*. slime promises a viscous enmeshment that both horrifies and excites. slime is a body, and the body's aftermath, the body's excess, its sticky, sickly traces. slime is an uncanny medium, cannot be contained or defined within any one obedient form. slime is a conduit. slime is *feral:* oozing, amorphous and multiple. slime persists, is a tactile reminder/remainder of the body that produced it. is a reminder of the ooze from whence we came, our material and undirected existence. slime is dissolve and displacement, invokes the origins of life in all its primordial chaos. what disturbs in slime is not merely our inability to bind and categorise it, but slime's infinite transgressive potential, its ability to encroach upon – and to breach – our own stolid fantasies of the limited and strictly bounded form. *my* own ideas. slime is *queer*, slime (dis)embodies the idea of queer – of trans – social contagion: it is not the riot of uncategorisable bodies that so threatens, but the idea of our own bodies – and the identities invested in them – as pregnable, susceptible and porous. not just men. all of us. slime *is* fleshy. but it is also spectral, a kind of rancid ectoplasm emanating from the body, capable of connecting not just one living organism with another, but the living and dead, the animate and inanimate, of stretching back into the past with its infinite libidinal elasticity, touching what it finds there, tainting what it touches with its many questing tentacles.

+

a reading at trinity college and a very famous poet says they like "certainty" and "structure"; the tensile strength of a line, the "possibility" of form. even by cambridge standards, trinity is something else. it has the largest financial endowment of any college at either cambridge or oxford: money rolls across the lawns like a bank of freezing fog. staring up at the cloisters, gawking my way across the courtyard, i can't stop thinking about the final and binding authority of certain forms and structures – poetic, architectural, social – how they advance and replicate each other. i can't stop thinking about that which form forecloses and renders *im*possible. the poet says that the quest is to sound "modern", and one can sound *very* modern inside of received forms. Catullus sounds as "contemporary" and is as "relevant" now as two thousand years ago. *is* that the quest? can that *possibly* be our goal? to create something timeless, impervious to the attrition of a long posterity? their work is clever, brilliant, but – the word pops into my head unbidden – *dry*. in which case, what do *i* want? what am *i* doing or proposing? a poetics of entropy and ooze? perishable forms? formless*ness*? which would look like what, for christ's sake? blank verse as some kind of sentient gelatin? well, maybe. in the reading my attention has wandered, and i am thinking about slime mould. slime mould is this weirdly de-centred entity: it is not differentiated into the tissues and organs that usually characterise multicellular lifeforms. it is a collective *without* individuals, no specialised parts, no articulated structure. an "us" not a "we". i use "us" in the poem, am "us" in the poem. after Ulrike Meinhoff's letter to Hannah Krabbe (1976, 2009), where she writes: 'when they say "we," they are only trying with their drivel to mold what the people think and how they think it'. "we" is politician-talk, snivelling and smarming. slime mould is the promise of something else, a squishy poetic commons. so yes, a poetics of ooze. where ooze might flow from the body in the form of slime or pus. or words. but also ooze as a scene and a state, ooze as a shape-shift, a sticky metamorphosis. myxomycota may behave like plants, fungi or amoeboid organisms at different stages of their life-cycle. i want a poem that behaves the same. i want a poem that rots, a poetics of rot, that ages and decays into the teeth of capitalism's monolithic use-driven temporality. i want a poetics of bodily and political senescence against the idea of mastery, productivity, endless fucking vitality and vigour, the grail of youth and beauty. i want a poetics of obsolescence and slime.

+

slug slime, i recently learned, is doubly strange, neither liquid nor solid, it solidifies when the slug is at rest, but liquefies when pressure is applied and the slug is in motion. clingy yet flexible, radically indeterminate. slime is what allows the slug (or snail) to cross the razor's rubicon, or crawl across broken glass; it reduces friction, insulates and protects. slugs are hermaphrodites, described in bestiary texts as 'mud vermin', a species born in and from mud, whose being is contiguous with their slimy environment. slugs can fertilise themselves, but they can also mate, and their slime carries the pheromone that signals their readiness. ardent mucus. leopard slugs are aerial gymnasts: their slug fucking takes place hanging upside down from a rope of their own slime. they entwine their bodies and evert their long, blue penises from behind their heads, braiding these together, fanning them out, creating a decadent chandelier of dripping spermatophores. slime is a sensual revenge against capitalism, which itself is a system with no outside, that operates through logics of incorporation and paranoid enclosure. formlessness is the feral *jouissance* of slime: against the implicitly excluding rhetorics of "community" – its multitude of embattled and competing subjectivities – slime instantiates a gloriously pervious commons. the insatiable *blob*.

+

not to valorise *blob*. *blob* has its good-cop, bad-cop elements: the way our hyper-connectivity fosters an illusion of potential threat to white, hetero-patriarchal supremacy; hive-minding and fusing us into a semblance of "community", the better to absorb us and to harvest our data points. but there are other *blobs*. my first and favourite was the character known as "Slimer" from the *ghostbusters* franchise: a hovering gobbet of genderless goo, bent on carnal indulgence and general mayhem. a repulsive "thing", whose mode of haunting was a carnivalesque production somewhere between a poorly trained puppy and Harpo Marx. Slimer was *feral*, exhibited that special excess of autonomy and lack of self-control so beloved by and prevalent in animals and kids. a glutton, but without the corporeal capacity to contain or digest food, Slimer smeared the waste of consumption, the wreckage of indulgence, all over that fancy-schmancy hotel. it was the logic of luxury capitalism, necrotised and skewed, wearing all of its crud on the outside. as a kid i loved its noisy, infantile being in the world, its utter unconcern with its ugliness, its total disrespect for private property, polite manners, gravity. don't laugh. this is serious. as a kid i favoured grotesque toys: the leech-faced he-man baddy that dribbled green gunk through its mouth-cum-suction-cup; rubbery bug-eyed boggles, melty-faced horror heads, gremlins and skeletons of all kinds. but even then i was uneasy, an interloper: adverts for these toys aimed them squarely at the male of the species. their special promise was, in fact, to incite abjection in adults and "girls". boys, i was learning, could harness external abjection as resistance and subversion, but girls' abjection was inherent, inert; plodding, passive. for boys, abjection could be dynamic and powerful, could be parlayed into an uncompromising punk stance, could even be a vehicle for radical change, but for girls it was only ever gross and squalid – ugly, where ugly is not transformative, merely invisibilising. one of my favourite films as a teenager was Troma's *the toxic avenger* (don't judge), where the humiliated protagonist, Melvin, mutates into a necropastoral anti-hero after being dunked in bubbling nuclear run-off by a gang of violent bullies. the *avenger* is capitalism's ecocide returned to sender, its very waste products repurposed as the instruments of environmental retribution. and Melvin's justice is also social: in meting out brutal – *and* satisfying, *and* gross – punishment to the bullies, the film makes an explicit link between the personal and the systemic; the cultural mindset that wilfully destroys individual psyches and entire ecosystems. which was brilliant. and Toxie is rewarded with the affections of a beautiful blonde (blind) girlfriend. here my enthusiasm wavered. even at his most deformed, suppurating and slimy, Toxie has agency. his abjection, in fact, becomes the vehicle through which he realises the masculine virtues denied to him as Melvin, and the script resolves itself in line with the normalising ends of mainstream fiction. and what do girls get? girls get to be pretty, girls get to be prizes.

+

it was the radical feminist Mary Daly who said 'the fundamental myth of patriarchy is goddess murder' (1978). she was talking, amongst other things, about Tiamat, the mesopotamian goddess of chaos and creation, best known from the babylonian epic, the *the enuma elish*,where she symbolises the forces of anarchy and destruction that threaten the order established by the gods. Marduk, who eventually kills Tiamat, is the god-hero who preserves that order. in her battle against Marduk, Tiamat effectively creates her own army by giving birth to monstrous offspring, including three horned snakes, a lion demon and a scorpion-human hybrid. you can probably guess how well that turned out for her. Daly's point was that the foundational myths of patriarchal society are predicated upon the violent subjugation of disobedient women. in the *chaoskampf* between

Tiamat and Marduk, female creative and biological power is exaggerated and distorted, figured in its most negative and repulsive aspects: Tiamat is abject, a *slimy* serpent, an unnatural mother to grotesque children; she is full of rage, she 'spawned monster-serpents, sharp of tooth, and merciless of fang; with poison, instead of blood, she filled their bodies'. the myth functions as both a conquest of female power, and the disgusted refusal of women's fury. you don't get to be monstrous *and* powerful, you get to be dead. i started thinking about *blob* and *slime* as both absolutely female, and completely beyond gender. as a new way of reading my lumpy, uncertain body, unsettling in its unreadable melange of gendered affects.

+

look, *blob* is defined as a drop or lump of something viscid or thick. of indeterminate shape, indefinite purpose, composite or unknown materials. *blob* is either "unfinished", or it is the waste by-product of more perfect, more useful forms. *blob* is failure, collapse, and wilfully so; *can* be a materialised revolt against the forces of heteronormative ecocide, but is also the result of those forces. *blob* might be petrochemical, toxic, plastiglomerate, a sick expansion of cells, that dark brown freckle stretching into melanoma. or else the mucal lube of living, slimy bodies. microbial life in the crust of the earth. superheated plasma. protoplasm, fetus. ectoplasm. gleet. *blob* might be a pleasure activist, like Slimer. or it might be the enemy. like Hannah Arendt's concept of 'the social': the desperate neoliberal subject, internalising the standards of those it desires to assimilate. in the words of Burt Bacharach and Mack David "be careful of the blob". is *blob* Valerie Solanas' anti-movement project – 'scum is not a mob, it is a blob' etc.? – where *blob* will neither accept nor escape the labels and trajectories applied to it, but instead incorporate, ironise, spoof, surpass, and layer them, in the boneless resilient flubber of anarcha-queer practice. *blob* is a bloke's *bête noire:* the fat, unruly feminist body. nothing to grab hold of. *blob* does not resist so *blob* is not amenable to force. *blob* is all the "no comment" you can handle, and then some. *blob* is not an inscription surface onto which you can write. *blob* is abundant, abundance. *blob* is insulated, padded and protected. *blob* is soft power singing to itself. *blob* as the squishy and amorphous forms of collective queer-feminist expression. *blob* as poverty of means, an *excess* of expression, an excess of *every*thing. predatory, threatening, an awful climax. the *blob* insurgent. the *blob* triumphant.

+

chorus sings from 'the blob' by Burt Bacharach and Mack David: "beware of the blob, it creeps and leaps and glides and slides, across the floor, right through the door, and all around the wall, a splotch, a blotch, be careful of the blob." ad infinitum.

+

am i *blob*? expanding, contracting, a weepy menopausal bag of stuff? Bakhtin writes that the grotesque body is an 'unfinished metamorphosis', a kind of a threshold (1984). *blobs*, composite beasts, monsters, and marvellous hybrids are disturbing because they never arrive at a fixed form, but brim and pulse with nervy, unnerving potential. in this sense all women might be monsters: pregnancy and childbirth already blur the border between life and death, self and other, troubling the margins that define – and distinguish – one body from another (Kristeva, 1982). but also because the female body is in a continual state of change. *slime*: neither solid or liquid. *woman*: neither maiden, mother, or crone. the grotesque is contrary to binarism, the collapse of difference. my borders are not sealed. my vulnerability is wilful and perverse:

not merely penetrable, but permeable, porous. the grotesque, says Bakhtin is 'the lowering of all that is high, spiritual, ideal, abstract; it is a transfer to the material level, to the sphere of the earth and body in their indissoluble unity'. so the more of this body there is, the more it obtrudes, exudes, spills out and over, the more "grotesque" that body: the menstrual body, the menopausal body, the suffering body, the poor body, the sick body, the debilitated or disabled body.

+

there are days pain renders me *blob*. i am aware that a frank admission of this pain causes a bizarre degree of discomfort in others. partly this has to do with the instrumental nature of "wellness" under capitalism, which deliberately conflates "coping" – a state of psychological, physical and emotional robustness – with "functioning" – the suppression of negative affects to the extent that you can operate as a worker, consumer and citizen. the neoliberal workplace tends to treat health – and mental health in particular – like a light-switch, an on/off proposition. if you're not flamboyantly immobilised, then you're "coping", which means your employers don't have to exert themselves on your behalf. over the last few years i have witnessed how the phrase "are you okay?" has been weaponised as a form of coercion; forcing the receiver to enter a false binary: how can you meaningfully answer that question when your only two options are "fine" or "dead"? it's this, but it's not only this. the damaged or disabled body also reminds people that the able-bodied status most prefer to consider as the default setting, is, in fact, a temporary and contingent category, disability being the one identity that *all of us* will embody if we live long enough. this *blob* has its uses, points to a queer-crip reading of the world that troubles the promise of a closed system – bodily, political, social – that recognises life as closureless, ecstatically unstable, and fuck the myriad segregations of your carceral normativity.

+

the ungovernable *blob* is also this manner of writing. an aesthetics of omnivorous accretion and excess, pulling everything it touches towards and into itself. it is the maw of practice, gape as method, the distended jaw and ravenous gulp of *feral* scholarship. *blob* may be asemic glyph and action spatter; Barthes' notion of an illegible writing, that, in its refusal to transmit meaning, calls attention to its *true,* as opposed to functional purpose, its material as opposed to instrumental nature (1985). it is writing suspended between graphic marks and gestural traces. it is writing that pivots between category and genre; writing that is not separable from the body that produced it. i want, i suppose, a poetry that behaves like Sartre's slime, something one cannot be rid of, that yields and clings. slime may be that portion of ourselves or of the other that we reject, but from which we can never absent ourselves. it is that which we are all emerging from and dissolving into. i want, i want, i want something wet but incendiary, like jellied gasoline. fire burning through to the bone.

BOG WITCH
(MY COUNTRY TOO IS SLIME)

nothing in the racialised ecologies of ireland exerts so powerful an imaginative hold as does the *bog*. for generations of english colonisers, the bogs represented a wasteland of negative civility, metonymic for the national character of an outlaw native populace: creatures who thrived in barren places; who made of that murky wilderness both a strategic redoubt, and a seat of high esteem.

+

as early as 1188, the *topographia hiberniae* describes the irish as a people who 'attach no importance to castles; they make the woods their stronghold, and the bogs their trenches', evoking a model of guerrilla warfare that would persist well into the 1600s, and indeed throughout england's long historical effort to "settle", centralise, and administer ireland. in our old friend Edmund Spenser's odious *view of the present state of ireland*, orginally written in 1596, and posthumously published by James Ware in 1633, the irish insurgent is depicted as 'a flying enemy, hiding himself in woods and bogs, from whence he will not draw forth but into some strait passage or perilous ford where he knows the army must needs pass – there will he lie in wait, and if he find advantage fit, will dangerously hazard the troubled soldier.' such are the conditions of asymmetric warfare: a warfare waged by a relatively well-equipped professional army against an irregular, though determined, local populace. in such a battle, strategy counts for more than might. guerillas who possess a detailed local knowledge of terrain fight a war of stealth, enlisting the very landscape those colonisers seek to claim as their most potent ally. in ireland's long rains the boglands became waterways: swamps, over and through which the accustomed gaelic irish travelled with ease, but which plagued and appalled the english soldiers. the bog is not merely a battleground, but an active belligerent, and it made the aspirations of military conquest difficult to realise. more than this, as a treacherous and deceptive site of instability, the bog reflects – or rather multiplies – those negative qualities ascribed to irish people. in the tactics of irish warfare, the english military establishment recognised – in concentrated form – the general ill-discipline, criminal opportunism, cowardice, and savagery they saw as endemic to the wider rural population. Barnabe Rich, writing in 1610 describes ireland as 'full of great rivers and mighty, huge loughs, such as we call meres in england, wherein are many large and spacious islands where the irish have many times fortified themselves against the prince, but are still ferreted and drawn out by the ears'. this last accompanied only with great effort and apparently at great expense, both financially and in terms of morale.

+

colonisers must represent the armed resistance of a native populace in such a way: not as a worthy or formidable adversary, but as a vicious and insidious enemy who succeeds only by means of low cunning. through this mechanism the occupying power seeks to recruit even its most punishing defeats as "evidence" of both military *and* moral superiority. if the irish are effective against the english military presence in ireland, that is because the irish are cheating; flouting "the rules" of combat as established by their more powerful and more civilised oppressors. disregard for those rules itself proceeds from a defect of national character so profound and so pervasive as to justify the logics of occupation and suppression in the first place. the english in ireland seemed to wilfully misunderstand that the land on which the irish fought would demand and facilitate an entirely different ethics of engagement, a form of combat that required considerably less command hierarchy or military protocol, that moved in patterns of raid and retreat, in sync with the living flux of landscape and seasons.

tudor, stuart, and elizabethan representations of the irish all attempted to remove them from any resemblance of civility. for Spencer in particular, this dehumanisation served an economic purpose: persuading – through the expedient of exaggerated menace – his english government backers to supply more resources, more men, and more funds with which to subdue the gaelic irish hoards. colonisers such as Spenser saw the landscape of ireland not merely as waste, but waste*d*, insufficiently utilised and poorly husbanded by natives whose failure to instrumentalise or master their environment served as further proof of their backward nature. again, Barnabe Rich sums up the english consensus 'i might affirm and confidently conclude that throughout the whole realm of ireland, what between the ill-husbandry of that which is inhabited and so much of the country again lying waste for want of inhabitants, there is not the third-part of that profit raised that ireland would afford.' dick.

+

Rich misread, as did Spenser, the complex sets of practices with which the irish interacted and made use of the natural landscape. singled out for particular opprobrium was booleying, from the irish word *buaile*, meaning something like 'milking-place in summer pasture' or, less poetically, 'livestock enclosure'. in simple terms, booleying describes the transhumance, or seasonal migration, of people and livestock, practised by cattle-owning families in order to take advantage of the lush pasture that grows in upland areas from may on. by taking their cattle out of the lowlands for months at a time, farmers could free up more ground on their home farm for tillage or for hay meadows. this rotational system required large numbers of people to move for several months to mountain valleys and remote bogland, where they would stay until at least september, milking cows and churning that milk for butter – a mainstay of the rural irish economy. it was this seeming-nomadism that so disturbed english settlers. Spencer describes booleying in terms of absolute disgust: 'there is one use amongst them to keep their cattle and to live themselves the most part of the year in bollies, pasturing upon the mountain and waste, wild places, and removing still to fresh land as they have depastured the former', reading into the habits of these rural farmers not a careful, time-tested stewardship of natural resources, but a recursive cycle of exhaustion and abandonment. in his fevered imaginings the irish are themselves a desolating plague, the harbingers and instruments of ruin: the land they pass through is soon decimated. in his diatribe against booleying Spenser's representation of the irish populace oscillates between the animal – pure, presence, incapable of the higher rationality – and the morally perverse. wild, yes. but *not* natural. a crime, in fact, against nature itself. feral. on this Spenser is unequivocal: 'there be any outlaws or loose people (as they are never without some) which live upon stealth and spoil, they are evermore succoured and find relief only in those bollies being upon waste places [...] moreover, the people that live thus in these bollies grow thereby the more barbarous and live more licentiously than they could in towns, using what means they list and practicing what mischiefs and villainies they will, either against the government there generally by their combinations, or against private men whom they malign by stealing their goods or murdering themselves; for there they think themselves half exempted from law and obedience, and having once tasted freedom do, like a steer that hath been long out of his yoke, grudge and repine ever after to come under rule again.'

the shunning of settled, sedentary existence along with the roles and rules such an existence engenders, has long been a subject of social censure, if not open hostility; such hostility is hardly exclusive to english planters in ireland, and it serves a particular purpose: by recognising only the limited forms of habitation and belonging that accord with settled notions of citizenship, the colonisers seek to imaginatively separate a country from its people. this act of dispossession serves to strip a native populace of their natural rights and prior claims to a land the colonisers wish to designate as functionally "empty". the extensive vocabularies of contempt built up around nomadism proliferate towards this end. what counts as habitation must be strenuously defined against mobile, indigenous populations; cemented and enforced through a language of legality that does not recognise and is little understood by those same populations. "empty" allows for toponymic appropriations or erasures; a wholesale overwriting of indigenous cartographies. lacking the symbolic status of citizens or subjects, the irish were anchorless bodies, wraiths and phantoms, composed of and dissolving into marsh or mist, living – to quote once again from Rich – 'like barbarians in woods, in bogs, and in desolate places, without politic law or civil government, neither embracing religion, law or mutual love.' a foul emanation of the land itself, drawn to barrenness and desolation by perverse instinct; incapable of those forms of "love" or "government" it pleased a sedentary english mind to recognise. a threat to the stabilising notion of the settled, inviolable centre.

+

here again is the *bog*, itself without centre. it had come to represent a disturbing indeterminacy that defied incorporation into the logics and structures of colonialism, and which itself challenged the seeming-solidity of english power. the bog dissolves and displaces, is oozing and amorphous, will not be contained or defined. it is not land, it is not water. it is a third place, both and neither. its signature manoeuvres are encroachment and breach. as such, it was literally threatening, but also conceptually unsettling, and it spawned its own abject metaphorics. for example, mud and slime are persistent features in *the faerie queene*, Spenser's allegory for the birth of a white english protestant nation.

+

monster-spawning mud is a general feature of *the faerie queene*, evoking the theory – then still current – that certain categories of abject animal life, notably snakes and vermin, were created through spontaneous generation, out of the earth itself, and through the inscrutable, insidious shifting of matter. for example, the nile-mud of canto i in the first book of *the faerie queene*, where 'old father nilus' breeds 'ten thousand kindes of creatures', such 'ugly monstrous shapes elswhere may no man reed' from 'fertile slime' and 'huge heaps of mud'. however, it is once again in Spenser's depictions of Errour and Duessa that slime has its most disturbing and suggestive incarnations. both figures are presented as concealing the monstrous parts of themselves; of crouching in dark dens (Errour) or submerged in/emerging from water (Duessa). concealment, slipperiness and irish habits of hiding greatly exercised english colonists, whether this concealment took place within the landscape itself, or was applied to the body by way of the glib (a thick lock of hair) or mantle. more than mere clothing, this last especially was politically fraught; just one of the many manifestations of irish cultural difference prohibited first by Henry II in the act for the english order, habit and language: 'no person or persons, the king's subjects within this land […] shall use or wear any mantles, coat or hood made after the irish fashion.' this injunction was met with indifference, and the mantel was still being worn when a new generation of english planters arrived in ireland in the late sixteenth century. it stood for the failure of earlier civilising missions, and the abiding barbarism if the native irish.

+

in addition to the crime of concealment, Errour is described as an 'vgly monster' who is 'halfe like a serpent', most 'lothsome, filthie, foule, and full of vile disdaine'. a hideous hybrid mother, suckling a brood of ill-formed 'sundry shapes' from her 'poisonous dugs'. snakes as avatars of both concealment and deception within the irish populace would have been a common cultural trope for the occupying english. famously, shakespeare conjured the association of irish foot-soldiers or *kerns* with serpents in Richard II: 'we must supplant those rough rugheaded kernes, / which liue like venome, where no venome else, / but onely they haue priuiledge to liue'. Duessa is also a repulsive hybrid, but her concealment is of a slightly different, less explicitly serpentine order. she is described in terms of stark sexual loathing: 'her neather partes misshapen, monstruous,/ were hidd in water, that i could not see,/ but they did seeme more foule and hideous,/ then womans shape man would beleeue to bee.' the idea of being hidden by water (as the guerilla irish were concealed) feels significant. Duessa's treachery is aided and abetted by the watery wilderness in which she dwells, and with which she shares a deep unwholesome affinity.

+

bog-w*g, Rachel W called me. *bog-witch, bog-bitch.* at the mainland school they called the jacks the *bogs*, a place fit only to shit in. when they said *bog* they meant ireland, they meant the entirety of ireland, as if there were no irish cities or towns, the whole thing a trembling watery membrane, a mirage made from rancid vapour. *bog-witch* would make me a mirage too. source of my punishable difference, site of my supernatural power.

+

Spenser's topography for the entirety of book i is a desolate and mutable wilderness. while england had long before suffered significant deforestation, this process had barely begun in ireland, and the imaginative landscape of *the faerie queene* corresponds to a high degree with that of the real, geographical irish countryside. throughout *the faerie queene* Spenser valorises productive or instrumentalised nature over the raw and untamed wilds, with their fertile moisture, untenanted woodlands, their winding, thickly reaching roots. such a wasteland is the proper site for monsters, and throughout the text geographical bodies and fleshly bodies are intimately linked. in the figure of Una, Spenser creates an idealised allegorical representation of ireland itself, but also a surrogate for Elizabeth I as head of the english protestant church. this complex figuration allows Spenser to endorse the subjugation of the irish people from the standpoint of both the colonised landscape and the coloniser at the same time. in Duessa, Spenser represents everything the english colonial mindset found fearful and corrupting in the irish "wilderness", but also the duplicity, licentiousness, and moral decay of the irish catholic population. she is a figure for contamination and seduction, a kind of living knot representing a riddle that mightily vexed Spenser and his contemporaries: did the irish impart to their landscape, through their wild, uncivil habits, the cast of naked desolation, or was the landscape itself a corrupting influence on those who dwelt there? Spenser gives this idea significant mileage in the hideous *view,* where Eudoxus, in conversation with Irenœus, ejaculates the following in response to the news that many of the rebellious malcontents in ireland were people of english blood: 'in truth this is more than ever i heard, that any english there should be worse than the irish. lord, how quickly doth the country alter men's natures!' see, in her repulsive, feral sexuality Duessa carries that very english fear of "miscegenation", then understood by the word "degeneration". further, her shadow is the spectre of sexually transmitted disease, ever-present in the mind of occupying forces, garrisoned in any kind of proximity to an oppressed native populace. these diseases are bodily, but also psychic, provoking a deathly corrosion of english morale and character. since long before the statutes of kilkenny, english occupiers in ireland had been attempting to forbid such associ-ation between the gaelic-irish and english settlers. an ordinance of 1351 passed by the dublin administration specifically forbade marriage between colonists and *any* enemies of the king, while the statutes later imposed a ban, based solely on ethnic grounds, on relationships between the anglo-irish and the gaelic-irish, prohibiting 'alliance by marriage', by 'concubinage' or by 'caif' (prostitution). the word 'degenerate' entered the english lexicon around the same time as the phrase "the pale" in about 1494. it would have been understood by the tudors, and certainly by the elizabethans, to have special implications for the racial, cultural, and moral "decline" from english norms in ireland.

+

this is certainly the sense in which it appears in Spenser's *View*, and he was by no means alone in his use of the term. Fynes Morryson, writing between 1617 and 1625, describes the irish as 'degenerate and barbarous' and 'infamous of rebellion'. during a period of both political and cultural centralisation within britain, there was still substantial anxiety around the erosion of english character, customs and language. as it swallows other nations and cultures, it fears the germ of sickness they may beget in its gut. the *View* attempts to detail this process in a particularly interesting and uncomfortable way, linking "interbreeding" and the intimate realm of childcare to a pernicious undermining of english civility. Spenser singles out the use of irish nurses for babies as particularly problematic as 'the words are the image of the minde, so as they proceeding from the minde, the minde must needes be affected with the words. so that the speach being irish, the heart must needes bee irish: for out of the abundance of the heart the tongue speaketh'. this is an incredible argument for the 1600s, articulating a profound link between language and emotional identity. it is an argument, furthermore, that pre-empts future generations of colonial projects, as well as the rhetoric belonging to various forms of cultural nationalism, historical and contemporary. whether intentional or otherwise, i can't help but think of this passage from the *View* when i read of Errour suckling monstrous children in *the faerie queene,* but in a more general sense, the bogland of ireland feels female – better, femin*ised*: secreting and porous, her iniquity betrayed by her synecdochic apertures, concealed, yet ever-open, leaking foul mutating poisons, the monoxide of irishness. in flesh and utterance both Errour and Duessa are morally unclean. throughout the 1500s it was by no means uncommon to equate a woman's open mouth to her other bodily apertures. for example this, from Henry Smith in 1591: 'as the open vessels were counted vncleane; so account that the open mouth hath much vncleannes'. in their material expressiveness, Errour and Duessa are excessive, shameful, and troubling. Duessa in particular. she is depicted as both emotionally incontinent and cruelly duplicitous, her tears compared to those of a nile crocodile: 'by muddy shore of broad seuen-mouthed nile,/ vnweeting of the perilous wandring wayes,/ doth meete a cruell craftie crocodile,/ which in false griefe hyding his harmefull guile,/ doth weepe full sore, and sheddeth tender teares.' female expression denied both ways as neither appropriate (civil) nor sincere.

+

dirty, Rachel W called me. amongst other things. and dirt was my chief weapon against her. against all of them. the time i found a dead crow and stuffed it in her backpack. the time i scooped scum from the pond and poured it into the hood of Laura H's coat. both the dead crow and the pond scum were aspects of my body, extensions of myself. "nature", in some nebulous and and undefined way, was on my side. "nature" deranged, in its most sick and sickening form. when seagulls attacked Rachel W as we trudged over the bridge between classes, she screamed and flapped her arms, blood running from the top of her head. everybody said that i'd "done" it. i half believed them. i used to concoct spells: seawater and menstrual blood, hair and spit. i cast in the hope they would choke, that they'd drown, that some kind of unspeakably degrading violence would befall them. it never happened, of course. at least, i don't think it did.

"ALWAYS ANGULAR, NEVER STRAIGHT"

in the 18th century northumbrian ballad, 'the laidly worm', a beautiful princess is transformed into a dragon by her wicked stepmother. she is only released when the king's son, her brother, returns from across the sea, and, recognising his sister, kisses the dragon as opposed to slaying it. having restored her to her rightful shape, he goes on to transform the wicked queen into a toad. yay, happy ending. in a later, scottish variant of the ballad, as transcribed by Francis James Child (1892), intriguingly titled 'the laily worm and the machrel of the sea', it is the young man who tells the story: *he* was transformed into a worm, his sister into a slimy mackerel. their father sends for the stepmother and asks where his children are. she tries to obfuscate by telling him they are at court, but he doesn't believe her; forces her to use her silver wand to turn his son back into a human being. this being accomplished, he has her use a magic horn to summon his daughter, but his daughter does not come, says 'ye shapeit me ance an unseemly shape,/ an ye's never mare shape me' (2008). and so, one has to assume, a fish she must remain. the father burns the stepmother at the stake. yay? i think we are supposed to understand that the latter version of the ballad is incomplete, and that the mackerel-sister hid from her wicked stepmother out of fear. if the full text survived, her fear would be assuaged and the logics of restitution and punishment could be carried out to swift and happy completion. of course, makes total sense. but i still prefer to imagine that the sister chose her piscean life, as i like to picture the princess' transformation into the 'laidly worm', not as a curse, but as a gift. and suppose the etymological confusion between dragon, worm, and serpent was also a bodily confusion? i read somewhere that worms are covered with tiny chemoreceptors, through which they detect chemical sensations in the world around them. or, to put it another way, worms "taste" with the whole length of their lowly questing selves. what must that be like, this radically different experience of the world? from a culture that privileges sight and sound as the primary metrics for knowing and being, into a form that makes possible a tactile and sensual immersion within your environment. an escape, surely, for women, whose world was – and to some extent still is – governed by appearances. hey, it's a thought. transformations and disguises, willed or otherwise, populate medieval and early modern literary imagination, and bestiaries are full of strange woman-animal hybrids. these narratives intersect with medieval notions of women as inherently deceitful, and with a general anxious preoccupation surrounding soft anatomies and squamous forms. yet they also illustrate how women might use disguise – even bodily abjection – to achieve social agency. now that's more like it.

+

snakes were commonly thought to be *slimy* and sinister. in the CUL bestiary, they are disproportionately represented. their various appearances bespeak a nervous preoccupation with ophidian malevolence. in the collective imagination of medieval europe, no other animal carried such connotations of deceit, temptation and sin as did snakes and serpents. the bestiary aligns them with death and bodily corruption, and with "unnatural" sexual and reproductive practices. snakes are explicitly linked to Satan through scripture, and around this idea accretes all kinds of unease – plain and fancy. there is some incredible snake lore in the bestiary, a favourite example being this, from Ovid, that 'the spine rotting, marrows of humankind do turn themselves into serpents.' in which idea there is a horror of physical decay, but also of moral and spiritual taint: the abject animal literally erupting from inside the seemingly intact human frame. there is something *slimy* in man too, something that can never be fully assuaged, a rot set in at his very core. it's a slippery, strangely circular idea, and you can understand why it exercised a powerful pull on the medieval mind: that a snake, originator of sin within the human heart, itself might originate *inside* of man. how apt. and how completely terrifying. another fun snake "fact": that certain serpents are 'brought forth in violence' and 'bring forth violence [...] both parents perish, the male when he copulates, the female when she gives birth.' this story in particular is one of many used to allegorise the faithless, deceiving nature of women, and the ultimately destructive power of their biological imperatives. a misogynist logic in which the CUL bestiary is by no means unique. indeed, the female form is repeatedly figured as a dysmorphic counterpart to male bodily shape throughout medieval literature, and nowhere is this more evident than in the strange, composite sorority of sirens, snakes, and loathly worms.

+

in the *liber monstrorum,* an eighth century compendium of fantastic beasts, the text begins with this surprising opening gambit: 'let each judge for himself the following material, because throughout i shall paint a little picture of a sea-girl or siren, which if it has the head of reason is followed by all kinds of shaggy and scaly tales.' as Frederika Bain notes in 'the tail of Melusine: hybridity, mutability, and the accessible other' (2017): 'this relatively straightforward description [of the siren] is coupled [...] with ambiguous descriptors that associate the siren with both "shaggy and scaly" characteristics, as though she were potentially mammalian or reptilian as well as or instead of fishy.

+

in this passage the narrator figures the siren's biformity as a metaphor for his own work, which he promises will combine reason — that which is clearly visible and comprehensible, like the human half above the water — with the strange and phantasmal — that which 'mysteriously hides in the deep, like the fish's tail.' this feels unusual, because biformity has achieved a kind of balance in the service of male art; it promises "something for everyone", a beguiling mixture of irrationality and restraint. yet biformity is primarily the realm of the female in medieval bestiary texts: there are many more animal–women than animal–men, and hybridity itself becomes a way to figure an assortment of negative female traits: mutability, duplicity, and – to quote Bain – 'the unequal yoking of rationality or control to the lack there-of.' while the lower bodily stratum of women – whether part animal or fully human – is conceptualised as bestial, even diabolical, the upper portion may 'be reasonable and amenable to virtue. this metaphorizing movement points to a common conception of woman as other— yet not wholly other.' other enough to require control, not yet other enough to escape the compass of that control. that's the difference, i suppose, between the artful and tidy biformity of the male creator, and the messy, monstrous hybridity of the female monster.

+

so enter Melusine/Mélusine. her legend, as popularised during the 14th and 15th centuries by the Jean d'Arras' romance, and elaborated in multiple subsequent traditions, begins as follows: Mélusine is the daughter of the king of scotland and his fairy wife. in her youth Mélusine entombed her father in a mountain (for ambiguous reasons) leaving her mother both heartbroken and furious. she cursed Mélusine, and as a result she was condemned to transform into a serpent from the waist down every saturday.

here again the lower bodily stratum becomes subject to monstrous change. i keep thinking about Mélusine's tail in terms of the *wuzho/marime* divide, a distinction between the clean and unclean for which the body is the most immediate map: in the old codes of "gypsy" culture, the upper body is *wuzho,* that is *pure;* the lower body is *marime,* that is *impure* or *defiled.* upper and lower-body clothes must be washed separately. women's clothes must be washed separately. spit and vomit are *wuzho,* menstrual blood is *marime.* and *marime* can't be washed away, it spreads through contact, and its contagion is both literal and moral. things that become *marime* must be burnt, or thrown away. where gadje hygiene seeks to cover and contain dirt; accumulating rubbish in bins within the home, for the old men, polluting dirt must be placed outside, as far away as possible. only dirt that cannot be removed must be contained. the hem of a dress, skimming the ground. modesty is not merely a mode of behaviour, but a spiritual condition. the *wuzho/ marime* binary proliferates a hundred thousand rules around ritual avoidance and boundary maintenance: between the upper and lower body, the inner and outer body, the inner and outer territory; between the male and the female, between *us* and *them.* to cross any one of these boundaries is to be hopelessly *marime.* to exist *across* is the worst thing you can do, or be.

+

Mélusine leaves her home and settles by a stream in the woods where, one day, she meets the nobleman Raymondin. Raymondin is distraught because he has just killed his uncle in a hunting accident. she consoles and advises him, and he falls in love with her. when he asks her to marry him, she agrees, making miraculous promises of prosperity and happiness for their family and his kingdom (which, in short order, she fulfils). her one stipulation is that he must promise to leave her alone every saturday, a condition he swears he will abide by. the couple is married for over ten years during which time Mélusine provides Raymondin with land, wealth, and power. as well as heirs. depending on the version of the legend, all or most of the children are deformed in some way, but crucially, are still accepted and loved by their parents. one day, however, Raymondin's family begins questioning why Melusine must have saturdays to herself and why she never attended mass with the rest of the family. Raymondin begins to wonder if Mélusine is unfaithful to him, and giving in to his insecurities, he spies on his wife while she is bathing. thus he learns her secret. in a fit of rank ingratitude, he then denounces her as a "false serpent" publicly. this sticks with me: his betrayal means there is no hope of her living a "normal" life again. it's a sad story, but it's something else too. the fable turns on the impossibility of love across the boundary, of marriage outside of your kind. what i hear when *i* read the tale is that they turn on you, however much you promise, whatever you deliver or achieve, no matter your love or your loyalty, they cannot abide and will not suffer any fragment of your essential difference to remain. you're a fool to yourself, girl, for thinking they'd stand by you. if you are "false", serpent, you are false first to yourself.

+

yet what i love about Mélusine is that despite her abjection (and rejection) she maintains a level of autonomy. her *feral* and figuratively snake-like properties allow her to negotiate the mortal human world and ensure her survival despite her "cursed" condition. her serpentine form, in fact, is literally the instrument of her escape after she is denounced and ejected from the kingdom she helped to prosper. Mélusine is, i think, a complex and powerful figure. a supernatural founding mother, her resistance to normative ideologies and forms enables her to both accumulate power and maintain independence. furthermore, her preservation of agency and influence turns upon her ability to manage degrees of visual access, her continuous movement between disclosure and concealment: a non-normative body whose otherness is accessible and invisible by turns. illegibility has been and remains, a reliable source of political autonomy.

+

as a for instance, anarchist cohorts close to my own heart: like the Invisible Committee, who practised what they called 'offensive invisibility' and tactical 'non-existence' to emphasise – and as methods by which to resist – the appropriation of identity for the purposes of control by neoliberal policies and digital surveillance. in *the coming insurrection* (2009) they echo our old friend, the martiniquan philosopher Édouard Glissant, in their discussion of opacity as a tactic for circumventing the apparatus of state power, and for preventing the personalisation of power in the hands of the few. they posit, rather, an 'éthico-affinitaire'. writing about the spatial and logistical dimensions of opacity, they state that 'every practice brings a territory into existence — a dealing territory, or a hunting territory; a territory of child's play, of lovers, of a riot; a territory of farmers, ornithologists, or flaneurs. the rule is simple: the more territories there are superimposed on a given zone, the more circulation there is between them, the harder it will be for power to get a handle on them. bistros, print shops, sports facilities, wastelands, second-hand book stalls, building rooftops, improvised street markets, kebab shops and garages can all easily be used for purposes other than their official ones if enough complicities come together in them. local self-organiza-tion superimposes its own geography over the state cartography, scrambling and blurring it: it produces its own secession.' this is opacity as both a tactic and a material condition; the way we might occupy physical space, *and* language, *and* bodies; the ways in which we might evade capture, and the ways in which we navigate our captivity. the CUL bestiary describes snakes as being 'always angular, never straight', the serpent excelling by 'a queer tenacity of life'. amongst the misinformation, this, i like: bent, tenacious, kinked into cracks and creases, surviving in the shadows.

+

and what happens to Mélusine? accused and furious, she flies out the window in the form of a dragon, or, in another telling, leaps into a river and swims away. she only returns to visit her children. in some versions of the legend her departure brings blight, famine, and destruction to the land. part serpent, part prehistoric bird, woodcuts depict her circling the towers of her former kingdom, calling down curses, her monstrosity finally and dramatically revealed. representations of her body fluctuate between forms, as with the 'sea-girl' in the *liber monstrorum*, she is scaly, shaggy, feathery, *and* slimy. her essential nature hovers in a similarly undecided space: is she a tragic victim? a justly punished trickster? a hero? a villain? as with Reynard the Fox, Mélusin's cultural shape has also been subject to mercurial changes: in some representations she is a fey beauty, an erotic enchanter. in others, her monstrous aspect is in the ascendancy. sometimes, she is figured as a benignly smiling mermaid, at others she is a devious and sinister mass of roiling tentacles and pterodactyl wings. *you* have met her before. if you've ever walked past a starbucks, you will have seen one of her more neutral and toothless variants. she is hiding in plain sight at the height of neoliberal culture, but she is a descendant of Tiamat, and the irish water goddess Danu, brought in from sea and free-flowing river to the fountains and pools of courtly enclosure. as in her story, she has persisted by "passing", by "masking". i think about this often, and about the way in which the "other's" ability to inhabit cultural space is often predicated upon various kinds of concealment. in academia, we cover up or minimise the aspects of ourselves that impede the smooth functioning of culture, the confirmation of status, and the transfer of knowledge. for writers, this same culture acts upon our work to eradicate difference through an insistence on standardised typography, lineation, "correct" spelling, "good" prosody, and through the consensus metrics of taste and style. appropriate forms, textual and bodily. above the surface, the comely and rational portion of our work. below, the sea-dark depths where the mask slips and the performance stutters. below is inconsistency and glitch. the body – of text, of flesh – that refuses to conform, and the work – in text and flesh – that the conforming world refuses. i think of a favourite poem, 'declaration' by Victoria Adukwei Bulley: 'if i live in the belly of the beast,/ let me beget sickness in its gut.' which is writing, thinking, and living into the teeth of empire. it is also – and the collection, *quiet*, thinks as a whole – about the work of self-effacement as survival strategy versus the tactical enfoldment of that self in the smooth-seeming skin of the productivity and compliance (2022).

+

or i think about Seneca, epistle 68 to be precise, where he suggests that when remaining concealed in surveilled circumstances, publicity itself may be a form of protection: 'certain animals hide themselves from discovery by confusing the marks of their footprints in the neighbourhood of their lairs. you should do the same. otherwise, there will always be someone dogging your footsteps. many men pass by that which is visible, and peer after things hidden and concealed; a locked room invites the thief. things which lie in the open appear cheap; the house-breaker passes by that which is exposed to view.' so i think about "the closet". i think about queer performance. i think about the "the closet", not merely as a suffocating vision of repression, but a potentially safe locus from which to conspire and strategise, hidden from state actors intent upon violent suppression, or from corporate forces determined to exploit you. i also think about the way neoliberal culture extends the promise of integration to those on the very margins it creates, a logic that renders both suspect and disposable those who cannot be assimilated into its liberal, representational regimes. "acceptable" others are integrated into a state's notions of citizenship: they endorse and perform narratives of globalised capitalist normativity and production: they want to raise families and contribute to the economy. further, the increased commercialisation of both sexuality and sex has created an ever-narrower range of acceptable – marketable – expression. if the other embraces bourgeois social values and is embraced in turn by wider society, then that enmeshment becomes the basis upon which rights are afforded, then the systems that strain to absorb us can argue that we no longer need – as a for instance – queer spaces, traveller sites – under such circumstances, what is left *but* to bide our time, beget sickness in the gut, await the eventual rupture? as Bain writes, evoking countless hipster tattoos, and the ubiquitous starbucks logo, present-day representations of Mélusine retain 'only enough difference to titillate but not enough to threaten'. that's how they like us, but we're the snakes up their sleeve.

+

Mélusine's story is the very promise of rupture. here, in 2023, a siren might figure not for what is beguiling and deceptive in women, but the ways in which we *all* negotiate disclosure, visibility, and access to survive in the late capitalist badlands. i love her for the shock of her big reveal, its destabilising vigour; how it undercuts and complicates all that coercive homogeneity.

i want to say: *when Mélusine comes out,* but it's more powerful and profound than that: she doesn't "come out", she is out*ed*, violently denounced, doxxed. and yet, she transforms what ought to be public humiliation and banishment into endless variations of quicksilver escape. i found Mélusine at the moment i needed her: ground down inside a wearying denial of my queerness; the daily routinised littling of my own unacceptable subjectivity, my own *neither-one-thing-nor-the-otherness.* through the bestiary, i became fascinated by sirens, whose name in english, evokes both sound and the body that produced it. in the parker library, i come across a depiction of two sirens, one predominantly bird, one more-or-less mermaid. while i had seen these hybrids variously depicted, i had never seen both aspects figured side-by-side on the space of the page. the working theory is that although most classical artists depicted sirens as bird-human hybrids, their affinity with the sea, and the cliffs from which they sung their fatal songs, led to their gradual transformation, so that in the *liber monstrorum,* they are already described as possessing 'the body of a maiden [...] from the head to the navel [...] but scaly fishes' tails with which they always lurk in the sea'. yet other depictions strand them somewhere between fish, snake, bird, and girl. what unites these different aspects of the siren is their musicality, their noise. in the parker library bestiary, the mermaid siren strums a small handheld lyre, while her winged sister tilts her head back, throating a song. the images are dynamic, so absolutely alive and in conversation with each other. i imagine them riot-grrrl harmonising, i try to hear the sonorous or discordant textures of their music. i think 'birthday' by the Sugarcubes, or 'pleasure' by Girls At Our Best!, or 'cannonball' by The Breeders. something ambient and trippy? something full of propulsive (and repulsive) energy? Sonic Youth? X-Ray Spex? maybe closer to the brittle and demented arias of Diamanda Galas? what compels me is that they *are* musicians, makers, creators. they produce noise, and noise is always political – politicised – inextricably linked to the struggle for space, power, and to acts of brutal silencing or repression. i think about noise in relation to class: how my own auditory and physical presence is read as disruptive and disturbing, unruly and excessive. sirens are twin symbols of allurement and destruction, their figures in folklore connect female articulation to the annihilation of men. sirens get their jollies from shipwrecks, their voice, to quote Marie Thompson, 'interrupts reason' (2013). their voice is the cause and expression of madness. picture Odysseus driven temporarily insane, lashed to the mast, desperately trying to stop up his ears. that's a potent argument for not shutting our mouths. there's power in that. the music will out.

+

Aristotle (yes, him again), believed that the high-pitched female voice was an important proof of women's evil and duplicitous nature. virtuous, brave (male) creatures, have loud, deep voices. in 'the gender of sound' Anne Carson writes that 'madness and witchery as well as bestiality are conditions commonly associated with the use of the female voice in public, in ancient as well as modern contexts.' (1992) myth is thick with a rotating cast of female antagonists who 'make themselves objectionable by the way they use their voice.' Carson cites the Gorgon's groan as a prime example. but i am thinking about the banshee, *ben síde*, whose voice is not the sound of grief, but the omen and the instrument of death itself. in the night i am woken up by foxes going at it like a pair of haunted pistons. in that blurry space between sleeping and waking, all i can think about is M, who died. M screaming. my own animal howl, sagging from the knees, still holding the mobile phone to my ear. there is something about a scream: *a fearful noise.* that which carries *no* message. a void and an excess of sound, a break in the data. like static, a kind of glitch, a limbo, a schizophasic techno of negative civility. the scream is what remains of language. i mean, what replaces it. of course our phantoms are noisy. when I think of the land, and of those of who have died, it is always to a soundtrack of women weeping. this downpour of polarised anguish.

+

the sirens have me thinking about my own voice growing up. my vocabulary was extensive, but my accent betrayed and mangled the words in my mouth. the lovies at the youth theatre told me to "eee-nun-see-eight". i thought of the annunciation, of the angel appearing to Mary. the angel's tidings were glad, but its aspect was fierce. my history teacher, Mr M, had just leant me a book of William Blake engravings, and fiery angels were much on my mind. the director of the youth theatre dressed like a cartoon beatnik, and while she was giving me "notes" i zoned out into an apocalyptic reverie. it was an old song anyway; the mainland had long wanted me elocuted for – as they said – my "own good". i was coming to hate the english language. imperative, officiating. it told us when and where to go, what we could and couldn't do; how much money we owed, what our allotted portion was, the hoops we'd have to jump through in order to obtain it. it told us about ourselves, our country. it silenced reply. the government ban had only recently been lifted on the broadcast of voices belonging to sinn féin representatives. i have hazy and indistinct memories of the BBC's most farcical workaround: Gerry Adams dubbed like a badly synced kung-fu classic. the irish voice as somehow inseparable from its politic, how politics is concentrate and bodied forth in voice. The collapse, as Carson puts it of 'the quality of voice and use of voice.' Bernadette Devlin characterised by english commentators and journos a million times over as "shrill".

and it's not for nothing that the republican magazine written entirely by irish POWs was named *an glor gafa* (the captive voice). voice is a weapon and a virus. on the telly, irish voices got to be testimony sometimes, but only english voices were weighted as evidence. rational, impartial. ireland framed and mediated, criminal and suffering. but *my* voice wasn't *even* irish; it refused to cohere into any static policeable form. they thought about voice as shorthand for a shared experience of national culture, as a receptacle for englishness, and as an aspirational vehicle, perfected towards some plummy upwardly-mobile ideal. how would i ever "get on" if i insisted on "wallowing" in the gutters of grammar and diction? they could not possibly understand. when home to you is transitory and shifting, then voice is more than mere identifying mark. it carries what home you have. it maps your movements, makes your journey manifest; it bears the scars of stored experience. more, it activates this archive, brings back and vividly into focus everything – and everyone – lost or left behind. voice is a story. voice is a summoning. for that woman, in her turtleneck and leather pencil skirt, my voice was a mess of creases and stains that needed to be scrubbed and ironed out before they set in permanent. i could never think of it that way. nothing is permanent. voice is frayed and patched; embroidered, embellished, and mended. like my walking boots, like my best blue coat, it's part of me, of us. english – "good" english – was trying to climb down my throat and evict me, to occupy my diaphragm, mould my mouth to its rounded vowels, drive me out of myself like snakes.

+

'caoineadh airt uí laoghaire' or 'the lament for art o'leary' cele-brated its 250th anniversary this year. it was composed on the 4th of may 1773. we have this exact date because that was the date on which Eibhlín Dubh Ní Chonaill's husband, Art Uí Laoghaire, was murdered in co cork, by officers acting on the orders of the local sheriff, Abraham Morris. Art was twenty-six years old, his specific "crime" is unknown, although by all accounts he was a bit of a lad, and seemed to be in the habit of flouting the country's suppressive penal laws, and generally rubbing the authorities up the wrong way. these laws include forbidding catholics from holding a commission in the army, entering a profession, or owning a horse worth more than £5 (which Art certainly did). catholics couldn't possess weaponry or arms, could not study law or medicine, and were forbidden from speaking gaelic or from playing irish music. these laws intensified the injustice brought to ireland by protestant english settlement, wherein they stripped the catholic irish of religious freedoms and nearly all of their holdings including land. when Art is killed his horse returns to the house he shared with Eibhlín, its reigns trailing on the ground, and blood on its flank. Eibhlín leaps onto the horse and gallops off to try and find her husband, but she is too late, he has died by the side of the road. in the first extremis of her grief, she begins to extemporise the *lament* over his body. people talk about lament as a form of mourning, an expression of grief, but it is more than that: a traditional form of extemporised oral performance in situ. a poem of white hot fury, where the lamenting woman – and in traditional keening it was usually a woman – is not just expressing her own sadness, but is using the public display of her grief as emblematic of the suffering endured by her entire community, and to articulate that suffering cohort. further, she's gathering and rallying those same forces behind her. Eibhlín's laments are singular because they lay blame, heap invective, call down curses, and incite listeners to retribution. i am always astonished by the lament, its swift movement through anger, accountability, duty, affection, and real terrible grief. from the curses, addressing Morris directly, but by implication also addressing the members of her community who are unwilling or unable to "fire a shot" on her husband's behalf, in defence or in revenge. then she pivots, she starts to talk about her sadness that she wasn't there to take the bullet for Art. she begins to address him directly as 'rider of the ready hands'. she moves out of that passage into a more elegiac mode, where she's describing both Art's virtues and her grief at his loss. all of these feelings constellated round this single figure. this is poetry as protest, and the body of the speaker matters; the way in which the poem is being received matters. we only have this poem written down – let alone in english – because its various fragments and versions began to be collected and transcribed around 1800, shortly before Eibhlín Dubh Ní Chonaill's death. before that it was passed down through the oral keening tradition, where it would have been spoken and sung in irish. that matters. return again to those penal laws and their forerunners: irish was first prohibited by law in 1367, and this law said that english settlers in ireland couldn't speak irish, and irish people couldn't communicate in irish with them. then you have 1537 with *the statute of ireland – an act for the english order habit and language t*hat prohibited the use of the irish language in the irish parliament, and later banned the use of irish in the areas of ireland then under english rule. then you have *the administration of justice (language) act (ireland)* in 1737. the act not only forbids the speaking of irish within the courtroom, it also prohibits the completion of legal documentation in irish and imposes a financial penalty of £20 each time irish is spoken in court in contravention of the law. what it would have meant for Eibhlín Dubh Ní Chonaill to have been cursing and lamenting in this very public way in her own forbidden language? the defiance of that act. and because she is lamenting the death of her husband in a language that is also suffering suppression and destruction, she's imaginatively yoking the two things. grieving Art becomes a way of grieving that language, and those traditions threatened by english protestant settlement. poetry becomes a counter-language; having a very different but no less powerful authority to those laws to which its speakers are subject. it's a way of intervening in language for those who are not afforded full participation in the legal and civic life of their own country. this lament begins in the body. a form of uniquely pressured speech, born of – and out of – moment, with its roots in extemporised oral practice, a porous form that suffers and seeps beyond the perceived enclosure of the printed page. how the body is a spur to this charged, collective iteration. Eibhlín's lament is full of suppleness and touch. it remembers the body above all else. and Eibhlín's body becomes a lightning-rod for protest. see, those mannered elegies are *memorial*. the lament is poetry's best self: *relational*, mobile and somatic. handed down, body to body, or breath to breath, across centuries. it incubates and spreads in sinew, in the soft-tissues and the long threads of intergenerational memory. like Jean-Marie Gleize says: 'revolutionary movement does not spread by contamination/ but by resonance / something that constitutes itself here / resonates with the shock wave given off by something that constituted itself elsewhere / the body that resonates does so in its own way [...] it becomes embodied in a musical way...'

+

i come to the *lament* because i wanted words for a pain not amenable to metaphor, the minutely laboured violence of it. for the double-bitted braining of it. i turned in tight circles inside the cancelled labyrinth of my anger. wanted words to quicken cudgels – crack – in the green wood of the hurley. to stop thinking of him, heat-sealed inside the coffin's pocket. walking in the last of the day's glare, this insolent solarity would split your eyes. to wake is

155

to rouse, is to rupture. i wanted to collapse the impossible silence which is, in itself, a collapse. they are well behaved. polite. patient in the face of my dirty, socially excessive grieving. i have put on *poet* like so many kerosene soaked hoodies. write an eejit's guide to catharsis. bound in human skin. at the irish studies conference we come to talk about the lament. our panel confides that we feel like frauds. we did not think of ourselves as *irish* until *irish* was painted onto us. kick-me sign at the small of the back. *identity* was not a cultural given, but a belonging we came to through an intense experience of *non*-belonging. to be bullied, evicted, abused, disbelieved. to have been, as we now understand it, *racialised by poverty.* everyone at the conference agrees that these are *weighty* and *important* themes. i am telling a room full of irish speakers that i feel the absence of the irish language as a prior loss. *prior to what?* to M, to Marty, to my father, to everything. how can i mourn in english? dragging my tongue through its foul cant over and over. what kind of grief, what kind of love can be made in such a mouth? our panel agree that we feel mainly exhausted. we are always explaining ourselves, apologising for our presence.

+

segue: the flowerpot snake is fossorial (burrowing), they live exclusively underground in ant and termite nests, but might also be found under moist leaves, logs; the compost heap of a city garden. their diet consists primarily of the larvae and pupae of ants and termites. they are tiny, often mistaken for worms, although their bodies are not segmented. they are a parthenogenetic species: they are *all* female and *all* genetically identical. they reproduce asexually, they fertilise themselves. this idea appeals to me. it undercuts the somewhat tedious gothic trope of snakes as avatars of perversion, sin, and decadence. it points to other kinds of queer relation: self-sustaining and refusenik. isn't that what we do, to some extent anyway? live by necessity underground? fertilise ourselves? foster a strange, queer lineage and kinship? i find myself sketching sirens, sketching Mélusines and Medusas. i'm at a reading up north, and in a public park there's a cod-classical statue of "Perseus and Medusa" where the 'and' feels horribly wrong: in what possible sense is a severed head, hung by the hair, an 'and'? that's not even the worst of her representations, which oscillate wildly between the hyper-sexualised – as in Luciano Garbati's still pukesome fauxminsist "inversion" of the myth – and deformed cautionary grotesque – as in Caravaggio, Reubens, etc. ad infinitum. the Medusa, lest we forget, was a rape victim, punished – by another female, Minerva – for being raped. because her rape defiled a holy site, Minerva transformed the Medusa's formerly beautiful hair into a nest of snakes, and any man who looked upon the Medusa would be turned to stone. her assailant, Neptune, who was Minerva's uncle and the god of the sea, escaped unharmed. no wonder the gorgon groans: the strained grammar of inarticulate witness. christ, i used to hate that story, but lately, in reading the Medusa through Hélène Cixous, I have found a kind of serpentine restitution. Cixous speaks of the Medusan body as jellyfish-like, fluid, elusive and ultimately ungraspable. jellyfish too exist outside of sexual binaries, reproducing both sexually through fertilization and *a*sexually by budding. although they are one of the planet's oldest multi-organ animals, the placement of those organs is difficult to define and to detect. for Cixous, the Medusa shares this disorienting biological structure: one cannot make easy assumptions regarding her genitalia, or her division into definitive body parts at all. she signals to diffuse libidinal feelings, to a form in flux, to a sexual ambiguity that poses a challenge to 'straightness' and to the heteronormative expectations that arise *from* 'straightness'. the Medusa's "hair" is a confusion of tresses and tentacles, twisting, entwining, and diverging. her "hair" has been variously figured as pubic hair or as a phallic representation (Freud), but for Cixous, it is their movement – a sinuous, indiscernible writhing or coiling – that transforms these locks from Freud's phallic snakes into a queer crown, signifying openness and sexual ambiguity. as Raquelle K. Bostow, notes, Cixous describes the symbolic queerness of the Medusa's "hair" as performing a 'weaving, braiding, bending, and wringing' action, which stands in contrast to both the bodily forms and lexical fields of straightness, aligned as they are with 'rigidity and virility' (2019). by contrast, the Medusa's "hair" incites a troubling 'vertigo', an anxious and thrilling instability in the 'hierarchical sexual binary'.

+

again, i find myself tilting transformative punishments on their axis, reimagining them as ascents, evolutions, and escapes. This speaks specifically to sexual violence, but i have also come to connect it to Donna Haraway's notion of the gorgons as 'chthonic entities without a proper genealogy". the Medusa – the only mortal gorgon – draws her sisters into myth and text, but their "reach is lateral and tentacular; they have no settled lineage and no reliable kind (genre, gender), although they are figured and storied as female […] the gorgons erupt more than emerge" (2016). in the myth of the Medusa, from the blood of her severed head, spring male heirs, but Haraway connects this blood to the "the rocky corals of the western seas, remembered today in the taxonomic names of the gorgonians, the coral-like sea fans and sea whips, composed in symbioses of tentacular animal cnidarians and photosynthetic algal-like beings called zooanthellae.' the Medusa's *true* children are living creatures of the marine tentacular – the corals, the octopuses, those spiders of the sea. she 'erupted' both psychically and etymologically, seeding new selves from her severed head. i like this idea because it posits a more-than-human connection to being in the world. it also suggests that writing – that knowledge itself – might be 'braided' or woven; connections picked up, dropped and entangled in strange tentacular relays, fuck the canon! Medusa as a series of snake-like perturbations or troublings to and within traditional modes of knowledge-making, traditional literary and academic lineages or positionalities. what this means for my practice is that rather than "foremothers" i seek a brood, a pantheon, a constellation of queer kin; rather than a line of descent, i want multiple ethical affinities across time, space, and species. in turn, the emphasis shifts from a striving towards "recognition", "reward" or "security" towards a fruitful agitation from the edges. too many poets, ossified inside their own legends: venerated, treasured, boring as fuck. too many academics suction-cupped to their positions, whose office becomes a gilded niche in a crypt. if there's more to life than marriage and children, then there's also more to life than tenure, to fellowships, to winning an industry prize, to being a book of the month, to getting your poem on the GCSE syllabus. searching for this "more to", a way to snake and slither. through crevices and snares. looking to spark something. trying to stay free.

'THE SERPENT LOOKS BACK AND RETURNS' (SNAKE EPILOGUE)

a friend of mine recently told me about Ophiuchus or 'the serpent bearer', a constellation straddling the celestial equator. in (the now largely abandoned) sidereal astrology, it is the thirteenth sign of the zodiac. it can be easily seen with the naked eye, although it might require some imagination to fill in the blanks. the constellation is described in a poem by the first century roman astrologer, Marcus Manilius in the following way: 'bending its supple neck, the serpent looks back and returns: and the other's hands slide over the loosened coils. the struggle will last forever, since they wage it on level terms with equal powers'. later in the poem, he describes how those born under the sign will be immune to poisons, 'receiving snakes' into the folds of their robes without suffering harm. a later, fourth century astrologer affiliated Ophiuchus with healers and physicians because of the snake's material connection both to poisons and to medicines. later western interpretations of the sign have tended to lean into the snake's long cultural association with evil, and to emphasise the 'serpent bearer' as engaged in an eternally unresolved tussle between opposing binary forces, or else the human figure subdues the snake by charm. both interpretations – to wrestle or to charm – suggest a quest for mastery. destined to be unrealised, perhaps, but mastery nonetheless. i prefer the more value-neutral designation of 'serpent bearer', which suggests reverence – maybe even veneration – alongside fear. this reverence is something we've lost in our imaginative understanding of snakes and serpents.

+

i had been thinking about this a lot, more specifically about the overlap between snakes' metaphoric and literal treatment. as a for instance: britain's war against the snake population of india in the 1800s, where the colonial government launched a bounty scheme, similar to that placed on wolves in ireland under Cromwell, in the hope of ridding india of an adversary they considered an even greater threat than "big game" animals. the extermination effort was geared not only to eliminating the snakes themselves, but to challenging the "irrational" hindu tolerance towards animals that had allowed them to run rampant in the first place (Murphy, 2022). alongside these formal extermination efforts, texts such as Rudyard Kipling's 'Rikki-Tikki-Tavi' allegorised their cobra villains as emblematic of india itself, figuring their essential nature and behaviour in ways that corresponded to stereotypical portrayals of exotic "orientals" – seductive, dangerous, and deathly. the mongoose hero of the story acts as a stand-in for the faithful native retainer, destroying both the snakes and their eggs in an act that scourges colonial space of those other unwanted or disruptive others (Kutzer, 2000). colonialism, lest we forget, is as ecological as it is political. it impacts environments and entities other than human; it destroys not only lives, but ways of relating to and being with those lives.

+

discussing this with a friend of mine they asked if i would be writing about Saint Patrick. i wasn't going to, not until they showed me a frankly horrifying article that equated a strong LGBTQ+ presence at this year's Saint Patrick's day parade in dublin with the "return" of "snakes" to ireland. i'd been cheering the advent of the newly-named *géilí* and feeling proud, not only of this emergent spirit of tolerance in ireland, but of the bravery of those who drove – are driving – that change. the article was rabid, regressive, and unutterably depressing; it had me thinking again about snakes, and everything that culture has glommed onto them. for those who weren't aware: there never were any snakes in ireland, probably not since the last ice age. their capacious function in the legend of Saint Patrick is as stand-in for any aspect of pre-christian ireland unacceptable to the fifth century church: what Patrick drove out was "paganism", itself a problematically baggy term for whole sets of social, cultural, and religious practices construed in their most negative and violent aspect. Patrick is variously credited with abolishing slavery, human sacrifice, and tribal warfare in ireland, and with "christianising" the country in the relatively short span of two-hundred years by "peaceful" means. i've been wondering lately what people mean by "peaceful", and thinking about those polytheistic pre-christian worshippers, whose pantheons included Badbh Catha, Brigid, and Danu. we know little of their culture, except that it involved matriarchal lineages and a degree of fluidity respecting sexuality and identity. the church that subdued and replaced them had behind it the weight of textual authority, and it used the abject animal other to story their banishment in vivid and triumphalist terms. in these tales the snake itself is indeed driven out, it disappears inside its christian iconography. the animal is lost, the revulsion it excites is all that remains.

+

what would it really mean for the "snakes" to return to ireland? for queer and non-christian persons to be restored to a more generous notion of irish*ness*; for an animal to be recognised and held as more than symbolic freight or convenient scapebeast? maybe i've been looking at Ophiuchus through the wrong end of the telescope (so to speak). suppose it's not the human 'serpent bearer' engaged in an eternal struggle for dominion, but the serpent itself performing an endless escape. never free, but never quite entirely grasped or tamed. the snake turns to face its handler with the level gaze of an equal. in its look there is extended both warning and welcome, both medicine and venom. it depends on how the snake is treated. snake says hold us with care, lift us to the light.

ON 'THE NAMES OF THE HARE IN ENGLISH'

spring has come to the cambridgeshire fens, and accordingly, i am thinking about one of my favourite middle english lyrics, the poem commonly known as 'the names of the hare'. i first encountered this poem in the Seamus Heaney translation, and only much later was i able to visit the original, which is preserved in the venerable yet bizarrely securitised space of the bodleian library in oxford. it forms part of a trilingual miscellany, rubbing shoulders with bawdy fabliau, romances, devotional texts, and oddball prognostications. the catalogue summary rather joylessly describes it as 'written by its owner' with 'amateurish scribal drawings and decoration.' for some reason i have always bristled defensively over 'amateurish'. the manuscript is said to date from the late thirteenth century, and to originate in or around the west midlands. i like to imagine it read in a thick black country accent, but that's just me. the poem's full title, which is given in french, is 'names of the hare in english'. it is composed of sixty-three lines and describes itself as the seventy-seven names you must say to a hare to avoid bad luck should you happen across one: 'and mid wel goed devosioun/ he shall saien an oreisoun/ in the worshipe of the hare/ thenne mai he wel fare.' [and with good devotion/ he will say a prayer/ in worship of the hare/ then he may fare well.] but why should you *need* to say a prayer of protection after encountering a hare? to answer this question, i first tried looking up this poem on the internet. spoiler alert: don't do that. you will inevitably find a slew of new-age blogs describing it as a "magical charm" against bad luck. which is cute. but, as it turns out, not massively accurate. it's certainly true that the hare has enjoyed a rich and varied symbolic life: hares were sacred to Aphrodite, the goddess of love, and there are numerous fragments of greek ceramics featuring Eros either pursuing a hare in circles or holding a hare (with varying degrees of tenderness). the hare was associated with Eoester, the saxon goddess of spring. and Boudicca, east anglia's famous warrior queen, was said to have released a hare before battle as a good luck charm. pagan or pre-christian britain would seem to have held the hare in high esteem, but there also exists a troubling fund of lore from the medieval christian world that treats the hare as an omen of *ill* fortune and grotesque transformation. echoes of such lore persist today in bits and pieces of superstition: if a hare crosses a sailor's path on his way to his ship, he should turn for home or risk being drowned; a running hare presages a fire; if a pregnant woman sees a hare, her child will be born with a 'hare lip'.

+

hares have been a central staple of witch belief for centuries. here is a snippet from the "confession" of Isobel Gowdie, executed for witchcraft in 1662:

i shall go into a hare,
with sorrow and sych and meickle care;
and i shall go in the devil's name,
ay while i come home again.

hare, hare, god send thee care.
i am in a hare's likeness now,
but i shall be in a woman's likeness even now.

+

therianthropy again, one of our oldest folk beliefs. and if such magic − as Silvia Federici notes − acts as a disruption or subversion to the social order, then the idea of therianthropy must have particular potency for poor or indigent women, who lived out their lives in the extremis of vulnerability, without protection, redress, or escape from a world in which they had no say, and no stake. such women were afforded the rights of neither citizens nor subjects, they were functionally and legally animals, and animals of a very particular kind: beasts of burden, their bodies harnessed without consultation or apology as sources of sexual, reproductive, and domestic labour. an act of volitional transformation, of embodied fugitivity and flight would have held an intense attraction, a means of imaginative escape.

+

back to the poem: in the always amusing *historia animalium* Aristotle suggests that a hare can get pregnant twice, that they breed and bear 'at all seasons' and can even conceive during pregnancy. this sounds bizarre, and Aristotle has form in getting matters of biology spectacularly and hilariously wrong, but in this instance he is actually correct: a hare can get pregnant when already pregnant. this biological peculiarity has led to hare parts being used as both contraceptives and — conversely — as a cure for cramps during pregnancy. it may also be the basis for a lurid piece of misinformation recorded in the *Physiologus*, that a man who ate hare meat would become 'a boy-molester' because 'the hare grows a new anal opening each year, so that however many years he has lived, he has that many anuses.' the hare was also believed to be hermaphrodite, switching at will between male and female forms. for this reason the hare was used during antiquity as a way to express homosexual desire. all of which is to say that the hare was a complex figure in folklore: often the embodiment of abject carnality and threatening reproductive power. the hare is said to reproduce without a mate, it has this prodigious and unnatural fecundity; it is Janus-faced and shapeshifting, fluctuant and other. the hare is queer.

167

+

the text of the poem is itself unsettling. something that middle english scholars have long debated is how seriously or how literally 'the names of the hare' should be interpreted. is the poem intended as a burlesque on superstition? or is it a genuine prayer against misfortune? as with the hare itself, maybe the answer is both. or maybe somewhere in between. take these lines from the beginning of the poem: 'bot if he lei down on londe/ that he bereth in his honde/ (be hit staf, be hit bouwe),/ and blesce him with his helbowe.' [but if he places on the ground/ whatever he carries in his hand/ (be it staff or bow)/ and blesses himself with his elbow]. consider the glorious absurdity, the slapstick physical comedy, of laying down whatever it is you're carrying and blessing yourself with your elbow, then reeling off this crazy list of names. for one thing is the hare just meant to sit there while you're doing that? further, the seventy-seven names both exceed and fail the poem's stated aims of either describing the hare or warding off the bad luck attendant upon meeting one. the litany runs from the obvious to the frankly whimsical, including many hapax legomena which repeatedly signal both the importance and strangeness of the hare. finally, the poem refers to the hare as 'the der that alle men scornes/ the der that no-mon ne-dar nemmen'. [the animal that all men scorn, and that no man dares to name]. this feels like an odd summary for a poem that just went to excessive lengths naming and renaming that very animal. one way of making sense of this is certainly as a kind of parody on superstitious charms. but i always wonder if something else is being signposted here? an anxiety about otherness, and about language itself? about our need to locate particular kinds of human domination within and through language? the unknown speaker attempts to categorise and know the animal other, to absorb it into his system of signs and understanding, to ultimately

168

control its perverse, amorphous nature and form. good luck with that. this control was a profound obsession during the middle ages, and i think it's this notion of control that gave rise to the literary genre of the bestiary to begin with.

+

one of the things i love about this poem in both its iterations is that, metrically too, it is an unpredictable escapist. in her essay on medieval animots, Carolynn Van Dyke observes that the poem's 'strong but varied rhythms suit the movements of an alternately wind-swift, lurking, scuttling, leaping ground-sitter'. the poem, she suggests, performs the hare: it follows patterns, but never just one at any given time. it shifts shape and guise just like the animal it seeks to represent or inscribe. i would also suggest that the reverse is true, just as the poem performs the hare, so too is the hare a figure for language itself, in its flights and leaps and swerves, in its many twists and turns. language simultaneously binds and expresses; it is a nexus for many kinds of power, it represents the authority of the law, it appeals to otherworldly intercession in the form of prayer or hex. 'the names of the hare' was written at a time when the english language was still in the process of being codified. how appropriate that a miscellany written in three languages contains a poem dealing with the capacities and failures of english to name and to know. what is special about 'the names of the hare' is that the poem presents the hare as an animal quite capable of escaping and breaking loose.

+

strange to relate, there is straight up a genre of manuscript margi-nalia that's become known as 'the rabbit's revenge'. these pictures feature medieval bunnies stringing up or striking terror into the hearts of those who try to capture them – think the killer rabbit

169

of caerbannog from *monty python and the holy grail*. for persons in the middle ages the 'natural order' was stringently delineated, so that any inversion of that rule provoked both humour and unease. human beings were at the top of the heap with wealthy human beings just below god, and peasants just above animals. what both the poem and the rabbit's revenge marginalia belie is an insecurity about humanness itself, how this is categorised and constituted. whenever i think about 'the rabbit's revenge' – and bear with me here – i am reminded of Bugs Bunny: his tricks, sleights, and schemes played out against the hapless hunter Elmer Fudd. specifically, i think about Bugs' cross-dressing: how he transgresses both binary gender roles and species divide to expose the performative nature of gender, the tenuous category of humanness, and to manipulate heterosexist desire towards his own ends. As Eric Savoy notes, Bugs is already monstrous, a man-sized talking rabbit fit for a medieval bestiary, but he is doubly monstrous – and is supposed to be doubly hilarious – for the ways in which he inverts the "natural" heteronormative order (1995) i have always been curious about how bound up this is with language. Similarly to Reynard the Fox, Bugs flips the assumptions about relative degrees of sentience and agency that are embedded within language and grammar. while Fudd mumbles, stutters and whispers, Bugs' speech is a bravura per-formance of wise-cracking and insouciant wit. he revels in verbal parries, puns, and jokes of which the less fluent Fudd is most often the brunt. Bugs Bunny is a quick-change artist. he needs to be, in order to survive. the hare in 'the names of the hare' is a quick-change artist too; it is beyond language's capacity to restrain or to absorb the living hare in all of its restless flux. the speaker is trying to get at the hare, to pin it down, to fix it in space and time, but the poem itself demonstrates that this might be beyond the capacity of mere words. ultimate victory will be granted, we read, by eating the animal other, and not – contrary to the poem's stated promise – by naming it: 'that thou come to me ded,/ other in cive, other in bred! amen!' [that you should come to me dead/ whether in chive sauce, whether in bread! amen!] it's an ominous sentiment, but a familiar one, an undersong of doom beneath the mad-cap frivolity, where the hunter determines to kill what he cannot control.

+

so rabbits and hares are tricky, tricksters. i can't think about the trickster rabbit without wanting to share the story of Mary Toft, the infamous eighteenth century "rabbit breeder". you might know a version of this story: that in october 1726 a poor woman from the town of godalming in surrey claimed to have given birth to at least seventeen rabbits – or at any rate, their mangled parts – a ghoulish hoax practised against the medical establishment, who had been only too keen to publicly endorse the "births" as genuine; a money-making fraud, soon exposed by Toft's social betters when she was taken to london at the request of George I. the story was salacious and sensational. it intersected with a vibrant explosion of print culture, creating an early media frenzy. but it's more than that. Toft's story is one of ingenuity in the face of extremis; a poor and powerless woman attempting to wrest control of her life and body away from the grim economic and political forces that governed it. it's a "trick" that could not have been played at all had not the "vulgar errors" surrounding both animality and the monstrous (poor) female body not persisted – in other forms – well into the enlightenment. the furore surrounding Toft's "hoax" suggests that while the idea of monstrosity had been domesticated by scientific discourse, a fascination with marvels continued unabated. "scientific inquiry" in fact, became the legitimating mechanism through which an obsession with the abnormal, the "malformed", and the monstrous was indulged. and poor women's bodies were so often the proper sites for such monstrous encounters.

+

Toft's claim was given credence, largely due to the prevalence of 'maternal imprinting' as a way of understanding the womb and pregnancy, where the womb was considered not merely permeable and susceptible to deforming or corrupting influences, but itself a site of corruption, the 'seat of capricious and forceful appetites that beckon foreign substances in' (Kukla, 2005). Toft claimed to have been startled by a rabbit in the field, and then to have craved rabbit meat. it was *this* story, of her shock and the unwarranted cravings that followed it, that first convinced Toft's local surgeon. to buy into Toft's story at all you'd have to imagine the female body as an an irrational place, defined by an absolute lack of control. you'd also have to imagine that the boundaries, not merely between mother and foetus, but woman and animal were hopelessly porous and thin.

+

the "enlightened" elites of the day hated Toft, and the ridicule that followed her eventual confession acted as a way for these same bruised authorities to recuperate symbolic power. by figuring her as lewd, lumpen, and knavish, they shored themselves up against the political ramifications of her transgressive acts. but, as Karen Harvey notes, these acts did not originate in a vacuum: as the cloth industry collapsed, and the poor came under increasing control from landowners who exerted their property rights over former common ground, including rabbit warrens, many labourers joined mass protests and trespasses, Mary's husband likely included. her fixation on rabbits, therefore, has a strong political meaning, however consciously intended (2020). the rabbit, appropriated into the body, not as food, but by other means, an image both of consumption and identification.

+

i have a vivid image – although it derives from something i've been told, not something i witnessed – of Ian Paisley, screaming about how catholics "breed like rabbits and multiply like vermin". which, quite apart from anything else, wasn't even original in the nineteen sixties: the first prime minister of "northern ireland", James Craig, had spouted similar sentiments ("they breed like bloody rabbits") to the working-class ulster protestant association some five decades earlier. sectarian claptrap, riffing off rabbits' impressive reproductive prowess, but that also conjures something of the depravity and tricksterism with which leporidae have been traditionally associated. rabbits and hares are "magic", parts of their body have a long history of use as charms or fetishes, while the animal itself is often considered an ill-omen. i am also reminded of the three hares motif that is such a prominent feature of medieval european churches (as well as buddhist temple sites in asia): three hares in an endless circle, each seemingly with two ears, while there are only three ears between them, each ear being shared by two hares. it's a tricky, puzzling, yet oddly satisfying image. i've heard the symbol described as representing the trinity. which makes a kind of sense. hares became incorporated into the church as avatars of purity or figures for the Virgin Mary, owing to the belief that hares could reproduce asexually. Rabbits, meanwhile, were said to symbolise a warning, little ciphers of unfettered sin. in the marvellous macclesfield psalter, which is kept at the fitzwilliam museum in cambridge, rabbits often appear playing organs and other instruments, dressed as priests, or riding to hounds. within the space of the church – engraved in stone, carved in wood – there is a ambiguity to their representation:

are these hares or rabbits? are they a warning or a benign evocation of the sacred? from their somewhat crude depictions it's
impossible to tell the difference, and this is also apt. they carry
something pagan with them into holy spaces, holy texts. when
i think of us as rabbits, it is not only as killable pests or feckless
fornicators (although we have certainly been classified as such),
but as something more unsettling and indefinable. i keep thinking
of rabbits' feet, dangling from keyrings the world over. luck of
the rabbit is like "luck of the irish". didn't do the rabbit much
good, did it? and have you read a fucking history book lately? to
draw out of the animal by supernatural means what is virile or
savvy, to discard the rest as not worth having. to appropriate for
yourself a portion of that animal's qualities or powers. rabbit luck
is the aftermath of the animal, maimed into use.

+

i have other favourite hare poems, poems that i love without
exactly enjoying or admiring. they belong to a strange medieval and early modern genre of complaint poetry: the animal
testament. the middle english poem, 'by a forest as i gan fare',
is special because it messes with medieval notions of human/
animal difference, bestowing upon the hare both meaning-full
voice and ethical considerability as she narrates the story of her
own destruction and consumption. the poem derives its authority
from two sources: firstly from the human speaker who introduces
the poem, and who claims to "overhear" the hare. this serves to
create an impression of verisimilitude, which would have been
important for the poem's first audience, evoking as it does a
prior performance culture. i also think about that long period of
suspicion surrounding words as detached from their speaker, a
suspicion that persisted well into the 12th century. words on a
page cannot be verified, can travel without their speaker, and are

therefore subject to manipulation and change. words on a page have no embodied authority, so here the human speaker steps in, vouches for the veracity of the animal's testament. medieval lyrics in which the speaker communicates with the reader beyond death were fairly common but extending this supernatural facility to an animal subject was less so. by broadening the compass of a received form to include a non-human speaker, i imagine the poem would have had an unnerving effect. uncanniness clings to it, the strangeness of the speaker doubled in being both animal and spectral. the ending is an uncomfortable summation of grisly though casual cruelty: 'as soone as i can ren to the lay/ anon the grey-houndes wil me have;/ my bowels beeth y-throwe away,/ and i am bore home on a stave.// as soone as i am come home/ i am y-hunge hye upon a pin;/ with leeke-wortes i am eete anone,/ and whelpes playe with my skin.' so i love this poem, but i don't enjoy it. it's a long piece, and throughout the hare is harried, finding no place of escape nor repose, hunted for the sport of 'gentilmen'. it is hard not to take on some of the hare's sorrows as our own, who have also been harried and driven, to seek a place of safety and never find it, coursed, and ran to ground. i think again about catholic families burnt out of their homes in the north, i think about traveller families, forbidden by law to settle or to shift. i think of all of our precarious working-class cohorts, ghettoised and gentrifed out of existence by turns. i think of the uses poor bodies are put to. it's a hard poem to read. most disturbing is the hare's articulate witness to the dismemberment and disposal of its body, and the description of this process as a "coming home". as if such squalid annihilation were pre-determined, as if the hare were pre-dead, never really alive. this is the lot of many animals. it is also the lot of many people.

+

connected, but different is 'the hunting of the hare' by Margaret Cavendish. this early modern work has more campaign spirit in it. it feels socially purposeful, aiming to persuade. in terms of tradition, it belongs, i suppose, to emerging enlightenment projects of close, sustained observation, applying scientific scrutiny to the external world. yet here the poem provides a kink or twist, because this scrutiny does not culminate in the exercise of instrumental reason, mastering all before it, but is deployed to spark profound emotional connection and empathetic response between the reader and the observed animal. the hare will not be reduced to the level of only a body, worse, to a metaphor for something "greater" than itself. sympathy is not afforded on the basis of reason, nor – following religious arguments – on the possession of an immortal soul. rather, the poem is a sincere plea to acknowledge the shared vulnerability of *all* living things (Fudge, 2006). i love, but do not admire this poem. not as a poem. on the level of language it feels – and there's no other word for it – kind of *janky*. yet my love of the text is sincere, because even its jankiness succeeds. for instance, the clunking cliché whereby the hare "gives up its ghost". there's something about bringing a non-human subject into the implied community summoned by the use of such a cliché that is, in itself, pretty powerful. it's a commonplace, a *goes-without-saying*, and there's an unconscious sympathy at work in that: the hare's belonging, its personhood or soul goes-without-saying too.

+

my brother and i are out walking, see two brown hares sprinting almost level across the next field, their bodies stretched as if straining against an invisible bow. the front-runner is most likely a female. if the male closes the infinitesimal gap between them, they may "box". such displays are often mistakenly described as courtship rituals or as dominance disputes between two males over mating rights or territory. in fact, hare boxing is most often conducted between an overly "amorous" male and the female fending him off. *so?* says my brother, daring me to turn this magic glimpse into one of feminism's teachable moments. i shrug. i won't. the hares race away into the poorly kiltered, shrinking spring. i am aware i spend a lot of time thinking and writing about animals as emblems. i am aware that the animal should be – and is – enough. i'm aware that our emblems are often so ugly. but i'll bet, along with John Berger, that our first metaphors were animals; that animals are not only subject to the meanings we apply to them, but our first guides for mapping meaning onto reality, the first to *make* our world mean. i think that metaphors and symbols can perform a kind of cherishing too, that they can be generous and grateful as well as reductive. maybe *that's* what i'm doing, trying to think about the emblem or the metaphor as a way of giving voice to the ungovernable abundance of the other. my brother is sceptical. probably because we are talking about hares and rabbits, and rabbits in particular have been done such a disservice by their representations. noted pornographer, pimp, and alleged rapist, Hugh Hefner, chose the "bunny" for his playboy brand because: 'the rabbit, the bunny, in america has a sexual meaning; and i chose it because it's a fresh animal, shy, vivacious, jumping–sexy. […] a girl looks a lot like a bunny, playful and joking. if you look at the girl we made popular: the playmate of the month. she is never sophisticated, a girl you cannot really have. she is a young, healthy, simple girl – the girl next door […] we are not interested in the mysterious, difficult woman, the femme fatale, who wears elegant underwear, with lace, and she is sad, and somehow mentally filthy.' let that settle a minute. then begin, slowly, carefully, concentrating on your breathing, to unpack it. 'a girl looks a lot like a bunny'. no. but her subordination is justified by a suggested similarity between herself and that animal. it's a perverse process: first, human values and moralities are projected outwards onto animal behaviours: so the rabbit fucks so furiously and litters so numerously because it is inherently over-sexed and "sinful", and not for the sound evolutionary reason that small, vulnerable animals would need large and frequent litters in order to ensure the survival of their kind. the animal can then be used as a symbol or allegorical shorthand for those negative qualities in human beings, is disappeared inside a dubious comparison. once again, dehumanising comparisons of this kind turn precisely on how little we value the animal to begin with. if a girl is animalised as a "bunny" she is not merely rabbit-like in her behaviour and personal qualities, but shares with that animal its status as (at best) a numerous and expendable resource whose usefulness to human beings (men) has a very definite expiration date. one of the main things about rabbits is their sheer volume, a teeming population of undifferentiated critters. that being the case, why would one scruple to value the life of a single "bunny"? or bother to preserve that life when it became burdensome to humans (men)? further, the "simplicity" of animals has long been the basis for a denial of their rights and personhood. Hefner evokes the idea (from Heidegger, although i doubt he'd read Heidegger) of the animal as pure presence, all mind, no body, dominated by its urges, trapped in a short-shelf-life present. obviously, playboy aren't interested in women who are overtly cerebral, artistic, unusual, feeling. *those* women are possessed of an explicit and obtruding personhood; not so easy to reduce them to the level of mechanistic sexbots or inanimate fuckstumps, to acknowledge a self, not *like* you or *for* you, but still abounding in unique, inherent value.

+

i bring up that odious coked-up scrotum, only because his

particular brand of idiocy lives at one extreme end of our met-
amorphising tendency towards animals. and i suppose poetry
might aim to move beyond those kinds of comparison, beyond
a suggestion of mere similarity and into the realms of multi-
directional analogy, full of strange affinities and associations.
it might also be true that poetry makes space for silences, for
the inadequacies and lacunae in our language when it comes to
the elusive and ungraspable quality of the non-human. i tell my
brother it is not that the racing hares *inspire* me to write as such,
but that poetry is the only passably adequate response i have
found to the animal, and to our related treatment and tangled
trajectories. something else: if the feral *could* speak, well then
language is already here, prior to us, belonging to someone else,
subject to *their* rules, *their* laws, before we ever get chance to use
it. i think of my poems, not as speaking for or writing about the
animal other, but acknowledging a shared problem at the point
we enter language, or rather, the languaged-world: pre-dissected
into documents, books, laws, bibles, grammars, objects that can be
collected, corrected, abbreviated, edited, and on into dictionaries
it goes, into baedekers, thesauruses, treatises, statutes, codes, all
of which control how much of this *thing* you have a right to
access and wield, that bind you or block you, tell you what can
and cannot be said, what qualifies as "speech". poetry – at least
the kinds of poetry i am interested in – might belong less to such
operations than other forms of language encounter, might include
the hare's leap as language, might extend less closure around the
idea of who or what "counts".

+

i have this nightmare: a skinned pink rabbit, coiled around itself
on a chipped white plate in the fridge. i open the fridge door,
and it's there. its dead, lidless eyes looking back into mine. and

then it starts kicking. more of a wet spasm at first, as if a strong current were passing through it, but when i slam the door and step back, the rabbit is jolting the whole structure so hard from within, that the fridge begins to move and shake apart at the hinges. the magnets fly off the door. i can hear bottles breaking inside. as a kid i was told that it was okay to kill and skin rabbits because they're pests. which confused me. how can *one* rabbit be cute, fluffy and vulnerable, while *fifty* rabbits are diseased, destructive, deserving of death? as justifications went, i preferred those that centred on bare necessity, proceeding from real, material lack. killing to eat, eating to survive, i understood. it's not valorous, it's not villainous, it just is, says we're subject to the same needs and instincts as the rest of nature. but this? like we're custodians or ecological engineers, providing some service? on behalf of whom? not us, so far as i could see. i used to have the rabbit dream a lot. as my time at cambridge comes to an end, i begin to dream it again with renewed violence. although i am conscious of being scared *within* the dream, when i wake it is not in the breathless sweat of fear, but to the immobilising slump of depression. i do not much go in for half-baked dream analysis (shades of Hughes and his burning fox) but what i intuit about this nightmare – what i *feel* – is that in some sense the rabbit in the fridge is myself. rabbits, i have read, cause something in the region of £260 million annually in damage to crops, businesses, and infrastructure. they are designated as a "common invasive species", despite being part of the landscape of britain before the last ice age. they were initially reintroduced by the romans around two thousand years ago, but only became more widespread and populace following norman conquest, when they were brought to britain as a food source. so "invasive" feels wrong, implies volition. they are, rather, an *extracted* species, carried here by the very human workings of conquest. to speak about an "invasive species" is both to subject the animal to xenophobic projections, and to elide the human processes responsible for their introduction into new habitats and ecosystems, whether those are the historical processes of feudal conquest, or its modern descendants: capitalism, colonialism. it's a nasty rhetorical squirm that allows us to ignore the social structures that enabled animal extraction, and to refuse the question of who benefited from the introduction of that species. this applies not only to rabbits.

+

but why am i dreaming of rabbits – of *rabbit*, rather – the raw, lean and flinty meat of it. and why do i feel the pull of more than sympathy? an uncanny identification? i'm not Hughes. i'm not keen to turn the fatal suffering of a real living creature into a useful metaphor for my own psychic processes. she's not a "thought rabbit". i wonder if she is a kind of revenge? for the feral presences i have banished from my life. and not just me. animals have become increasingly absent from the lives of many modern western publics, while at the same time we are inundated and surrounded – fair saturated – by animal imagery: cartoons, logos, toys, mascots, adverts, postcards, costumes, cute christmas decorations. these images don't help us remember the real animal, they are an aide to ignorance, to a generalised forgetting. it's easter, i suppose, lent term and its parade of kitschy chocolate "bunnies". these rabbits multiply too. and signify wildly, hectically. on my way into work i make a point of counting rabbits: on tote bags and t-shirts, on supermarket and train station hoardings, on the side of kids' juice cartons and bags of sweeties, on the soft furnishings in the john lewis homeware department as i cut through lion's yard to the other side of town. the boxing hares logo repeats nine times, under the legend *fighting animal testing*. and oh the rabbits. so many rabbits: stylised geometric hipster rabbits; cute, cuddly plush rabbits; goofy simplified special-offer rabbits; corporate clip-art wankers' paradise rabbits; elegant art-deco rabbits; beloved foil-wrapped chocolate rabbits, my good friend's tattoo of two dead rabbits; *vegan jihad* graffiti rabbits, on and on. i suppose i could have performed the same experiment with any animal. my friend says rabbits are *not* disappearing, how can they be? there are over 40 million of them. elsewhere in the world the diversity of life is continuously shrinking, with (conservative estimate) 27,000 species lost every year. we see rabbits all the time, he says, *they're fuckin' everywhere.* alright, then not disappeared exactly, but denied, shut out. he shrugs: *you know, animal testing for cosmetic purposes has been illegal in the uk since 1998?* of course i know, i snap back. he shoots me some more rabbit facts: did i know that the "sexy" cadbury's caramel bunny was voiced by *everyone's favourite lesbian, Miriam Margolyes.* i did *not* know that. we have a long discussion about how that advert was simultaneously apt and fucked, but i feel twitchy. my dream is with me, the tackiness of skinned meat, the staring eye unable to close. i shut *my* eyes, but before them march an endless parade of imaginary rabbits: from Roger Rabbit through Harvey, to the cadbury's bunny, and Frank from *donnie darko.* sexy rabbits, silly rabbits, sleek rabbits, skittish rabbits, sinister rabbits, cunning rabbits, lucky rabbits, plucky rabbits, greedy rabbits, savvy rabbits, on and on. figures for this, for that. until finally it hits me, and i say: it's because they mean but they don't matter.

+

and i find myself gesticulating, waving my hands, banging on about Ian Paisley, and – of all people – Kate sodding Clanchy. my friend looks spooked, like *how-did-we-get-here?* but i'm ranting and ranting, and i think i might cry. he keeps saying *mate, calm down.* in an increasingly panicked voice, and flicking his eyes around helplessly, like he wants to be rescued from this hysterical, bellowing fruitcake. which only serves to wind me up more. and i'm trying to explain. it's like women. it's like being poor. it's like being poor women. it's being a *mob*, a *tribe*, a *swarm*, a *herd*, whom they can't tell apart; on and through whose bodies the marks of their class are stamped 'like letters in a stick of rock' (Clanchy). who are greedy, "surplus eaters". a homogenous white gloop of common-or-garden ugliness. not special. not rare. nothing. worth nothing in themselves, but oh, such a convenient crutch for white supremacy, a useful structural rebuttal: how much we are "suffering", "struggling", wheeling us out like prizes on a shit seventies game-show going "look at the poor white kids left behind" when they couldn't give a toss the rest of the time, shoving us in the faces of minoritised groups and their advocates, shoring up their institutionally racist halfwittedness with the mortar of poor white bodies. and because there are so many of us, and because we have no distinct identity at all, it doesn't matter what happens to any single one of us. and because we don't matter, we can mean, we can be that structural rebuttable, rhetorical flourish, law-and-order bête-noire, amorphous entity, stuff of nightmares: "the white working classes", expendable, disposable.

+

and breathe out. i tell him, look, it's like this: competing and contradictory meanings proliferate around rabbits because they don't matter, you see? they're voids, vague animal shapes, mass-produced, reproduced; they've no identity of their own, no prior "self" to be displaced. and i think maybe it's the same for us, politically, yes, but also inside of art and culture: we're props, *types*, tropes. can be troped, aped, performed. how they do us pikey in different voices. *alright,* he says, *but that's not just rabbits, is it? that's all animals.* and this is not news to me, and i've written about this before, so why am i getting so upset now? it's the dream. it's how old this stuff is. *for instance?* and i find myself talking about the 1572 *vagrancy act*, and the 1598 *poor law*, its punitive control of – especially – the itinerant poor, themselves figured as an "invasive species". the *poor law* initiated legal deportation for crimes such as vagrancy; it emerged from and cemented a deep repulsion for this licentious, promiscuous population of 'roguish travelling people, which in their common whoredome, resemble lawlesse beastes' (Michael Sparke, 1612). such "vagrants" were commonly compared to drones, wasps, and most often to rabbits, classifications that emphasise not merely their animality, but an abject absence of reason, order, or restraint. and if rabbits could be figuratively deployed to stand for us itinerant poor, then the itinerant poor themselves also became similes and metaphors. for example, of disorder in the church, with non-resident clergy being described as vagrants for having no fixed parish. or else we were simply symbols of social and political decay, "caterpillars of the commonwealth", profligate, idle yet sturdy, living off the sweat from others' brows. the poor were legislated against, of course, but we were also imagined against. read Spenser if you want an eyeful of that.

+

but why am i dreaming of skinned rabbits? there was a denial, i suppose, somewhere along the line, of grisliness and hurt. maybe because i write about poverty without naming or acknowledging exactly what that involved. because i can't talk about how we lived, and i can't address what happened to me. because i've become part of this torrent of shit that erects "working-class" like some unassailable moral category, some monolithic identity whose borders must be continually confirmed, affirmed, and policed. because i've turned *myself* into a cartoon, because that's how i live, that's what i live *off*. because i want to make space for the animal, for those who didn't make it, for those who weren't reckoned to be worth saving. because when i say *animal* i mean rabbits and poor people and travellers and women too. i mean the animal*ised*. i mean i am *not* special or different just because i've got a desk in an office and a steroidal vocabulary, and yet my humanity is afforded me on precisely that basis. that's wrong, so wrong. i say to my friend, what if there's a litany of names for the magic of us? what if language can perform that restitution? like i could language us all back to life, to glory. is that the work of poetry? *i dunno, doc, you tell me.*

THE CABINET /
THE CLOSET

it's not that i don't like it, but what is it? this, my dear friend.
meaning, that this writing too is a composite beast, an inelegant
compromise, a motley of textual forms crudely sutured, and that
it will wind up pleasing nobody very much. an essay is an essay.
a poem is a poem. not lyric, not strictly academic, not properly
confessional. *this* is some third thing. adulterated. mongrel. i've
no argument to make. but i tried for months to write a collection
of self-contained, concise, connected essays. i read collections
by other poets. some of these i loved. some were slinky little
grimoires of "connection" and "catharsis". they made me want to
puke. either way, i couldn't reproduce that fluency, that confidence,
that clarity. not even if i wanted to. and i don't know that i wanted
to. here, i hit a wall. the wall coincides with an ebb in both energy
and self-belief. it makes it back to me that a writer i thought of
as basically an ally has been describing my recent work to others
as "pretentious marxist word-salad", and that's not nice to hear.
more than this, while i hide among the manuscripts, my life as
i have known it begins to unravel. i'm living out of a suitcase,
unsure where *home* is, feeling alternately lost and suffocated. an
animal in a trap will chew off its own leg to get free. i can't even
muster the guts to make one poxy decision. i just stand there – not
unlike a lamped rabbit – mesmerised, paralysed. how i feel about
myself bleeds into how i feel about my work, both poetry and
prose. on a good day, i'm the head of my own experiment into
the elasticity and limits of language, looking for something that's
neither rhetoric or semiosis, but both, or more, or else. there have
been few such good days lately. my friend says i should write it
down, a kind of *ars poetica,* or manifesto, what it is i think i'm
doing. okay.

fuck catharsis: we shouldn't have to find ways to endure an unacceptable reality, if art is helping you to endure, is making you feel
comfortable, seen, recognised and heard inside of a system that
wants to destroy you, then that's not art at all, that's propaganda.
i want to say that writing isn't an adequate or lasting salve to the
wounds we receive in the world. feeling "better" is not a substitute
for active, collective social change. i want a writing that might
create the conditions in consciousness that will, in time, permit
their expression inside of the real. or, as Audre Lorde writes, a
poetry that will 'give name to the nameless so it can be thought'
(1985). i'll fail. but i won't go down making a bland peaceable
art that "connects" with people in ways that elide the potentially
fatal extent of our difference. my relationship with my readers
isn't meant to be benign. we're not neighbours, we're not mates.
and i'm not a branch of the fucking service industry. i'm not a
stop-gap, a less-expensive form of therapy, a substitute for equal
access to mental health provision. this isn't entertainment. i'm
not writing to ease their discomfort. or my own. all of this, and i
want to say something about the *taymouth hours,* an illuminated
devotional text from the 14th century, intended for use by a single
elite reader. i want to show people the leering gremlin faces in the
borders of that sacred text, and say hey, the myriad grotesqueries
that pepper the margins of medieval religious manuscripts are
profane to a purpose: their presence poses a moral dilemma, they
dramatise the encroachments and temptations of the material
world; they require of their reader a determined choice, a conscious and deliberate reinvestment of attention in the spiritual
message of their text. i want a writing like that, that inundates
and overwhelms, that keeps shoving the world in your face, its
degradations and assaults, its banalities and barbarisms. i want a
writing that extracts something (sweat, blood, the piss, non-trivial

effort), and that doesn't offer some smug monolithic insight on how best to accommodate that shit. it's not art's job – and it's certainly not poetry's – to parlay pain into consolation. i want thoughts and feelings that cannot be assimilated, beautified, or eased. i am not a believer in frictionless catharsis, in art or in life. who says our task is to translate the difficult stuff of raw experience into some ideal of emotional expressiveness, to mould our losses into readily accessible codes of plain statement? i hate the empathetic sigh, where catharsis is suspiciously akin to absolution, provides a release, lets us off the hook. the deep swell of feeling a poem prompts may *seem* profound – momentous even – but it is interior, entirely subjective, the opposite of true sympathy, true solidarity. this kind of poetry, and the idea that it "connects" people through a golden thread of fellow feeling, works to conceal those inequalities that divide us and contour every aspect of our lives. i *hate* catharsis, because it makes a fetish of working-class resilience; it ties that suffering to a marketable performance of identity, where your pain has meaning and value only in so far as it elicits that sweeping emotional response in your audience. and writing the poem may help us – great, better out than in – but its efficacy in challenging the attitudes and conditions that produce those feelings is limited. and it's limited by language as much as by the political and social systems that administer us. i want something in the text that must be borne with and surmounted; i want to signpost the failures and limitations of a language that always seems to resist or evict me.

+

that's not an answer. okay. should i talk about the innumerable, market-driven privatisations of language, corporate and legal? from libel and copyright laws to the restrictions placed on free speech by acts of parliament; through censorship and trademarking, the banning of some texts altogether? language is recruited in the service of its own suppression, and isn't that just the most fucked up thing you can think of? what about schooling as a strategy of enclosure, stamping out language as a lived oral commons? what about the privileging of received pronunciation over accent and dialect, and the sorry standardisation of literary forms? if i want my writing to be anything, i want it to be anything but *that*. i want to show that this material with which we work is not blameless or neutral. i want to make manifest our continual, exhausting negotiation with and within language; with and within capitalism. and i'm trying to get to the other side of that – to find a way of using language and form that doesn't feel like violence or betrayal.

+

small voice hisses *hypocrite!* i talk a good game, but i'm here, aren't i? John Berger says that captive or displayed animals lose a vital component of their essential animality; kept to perpetuate the illusion of "nature". the physically close yet conceptually distant animal. *and that's you, that is.* collected, exhibited, ultimately discarded from the cambridge wunderkammer. Jean Baudrillard calls such collecting 'an exertion of power or dominance', one that is immeasurably more successful than human attempts to control *living* things (1996).

+

my friend says that university-as-wunderkammer is not an especially useful metaphor. perhaps he's right. at the very least, it might be incomplete. maybe i am agitated more by the representational model of inclusion at work across academia, the arts and culture, where we are never allowed to stand for ourselves, but must be made to "represent" or signify, for cohorts, voices, positionalities. or, as another friend wryly commented about a panel on which we both sit: *they've got a brown one, a black one, a poor one and a queer one.* they don't expect us to do anything, just sit there and look diverse. we talk about changing the masthead to the slogan THIS RAINBOW COALITION WILL FUCK YOUR SHIT UP! but of course that won't happen. i was reading about how for early modern people the idea of accepting an animal or plant on its own merits was 'almost unthinkable' (Peter Daly, 1979). as evidence, take the popularity of the *hieroglyphica*, which claims to reveal the meaning behind egyptian hieroglyphs, but that mixes in a good deal of wacky (often wrong) ancient natural history. it was supposedly written by the egyptian magus Horapollo Niliacus in the fourth century; it contains hundreds of allegorical emblems said to have been used by pharaonic scribes to depict both natural and moral aspects of the world. translated into greek in 1505, it cast a long shadow, continuing to influence much of western iconography from the sixteenth through nineteenth centuries. tellingly, "Horapollo" writes that 'animals were the living characters in the language of the creator.' this was the prevailing view throughout the early modern period, and the logic through which wunderkammers were assembled and displayed. animals were mere hieroglyphics of god's glory and mysterious workings (Finden, 1994). collectors went to great lengths to acquire rare objects which were exotic, or grotesque. as Stephan Asma notes 'curiosity cabinets had a purpose, an underlying but persistent agenda: to show that god is prolific, prodigious, and ingenious.' while objects of natural wonder demonstrated both the diversity and power of god, oddities and grotesques were evidence of divine retribution (2003). impairment of any kind had such powerful religious and social connotations in both the medieval and early modern period. it's not that disabilities were thought to be caused by sin so much, as impaired people themselves were used as either community scapegoats or moral metaphors, often being described as dupes or tools of the devil, resembling more monsters than men. *so what?* says my friend. so, aren't *we* collected to a purpose, to support an "underlying agenda" too? not about the omnipotence of god, but about the cultural ascendancy of rainbow-capitalism. *yeah... you're reaching, mate.*

+

so i'm reaching, but i am also genuinely attempting to think about what the university *is*, why i'm here, and what that means for a poetics formed far outside of its walls. as friends, family and colleagues have all been quick to point out, i did this to myself, i came here willingly and on purpose. *are you sure it's a cabinet, and not a closet?* well, could the university be that space of tactical concealment or retreat? maybe even the only space where i can effectively negotiate between overlapping and contradictory demands? the university not as a space of "outness" or acceptance exactly, but oscillation, between disclosure and restraint, visibility and invisibility. not only in terms of sexuality and gender, but in terms class, culture, impairment, etc. think of the university as that space inside of which i am able to feel, simultaneously, the need to belong and the impossibility of belonging. the space that makes my queerness – my *feral*ness – manifest.

+

neither queerness *nor* feralness can constitute themselves, forced to exist only in reference to a stable and conforming centre. this is the violence of "*queer!*" figuring queer as the result of unspecified damage; queer itself as damage. they fill it up with melancholy, a yearning to establish some centre of our own. *this* is the cavernous quality of queer desire, how we can only understand ourselves as whole in the act of reaching towards another, in that generous extension of affection, the need to form and confirm a compassionate commons. the queer is like feral, a mode of being imperfectly held within language; that cuts across and partakes of multiple categories of vexed belonging. not merely other, but colliding all aspects of otherness. both and neither, queer finds no ideal expression of solidarity, no true *home*, in any one territory or lexical field. they used to shout *"queer!"* at me. where *"queer!"* concentrates all their phobic tendencies in one place. a word for the way in which class, ethnicity, and sexuality complicate or undermine each other. where my shaved head is a blank slate onto which anyone is free to inscribe aspects of otherness. where i gather to myself an entire global history of negative assumption: indiscriminate, unnatural, disgusting, diseased, repressed, hysterical, mad. can the university provide a place to grapple and to strategise through these thoughts, a counter-space inside of wider society, as it attempts to evict *or* recruit me according to what is politically expedient, or according to the logics of the market?

+

"queer!" takes place within language too. is how they shrink our supple and excessive otherness, little it *inside* of language. *"queer!"* is an abundance that we apprehend as lack because the words that would have allowed us to experience it as a positive quality have been taken away from us. replaced with *"queer!"* which is that silencing, which is the verdict and the sentence. i have come here to think these thoughts. nowhere else makes room for them. to think through and *with* a literary and representational history of non-normative forms. to find a way, not to "reclaim" queerness, or the sleight/slight of *feral,* but to learn to incorporate them, to breach and multiply them, to rupture and loop them. which is something more powerful than enthusiastic welcome or perfect belonging.

i am not fooled. i operate under few illusions. this is not my place. i will only ever be an interloper, an infiltrator; suspect synanthrope, feral scholar, a "poundland academic", a bad writer. i will be doubted, and i will doubt myself. but i'll stick it out. i'll stay. let's not valorise that, the grubby, necessary work of persistence, but let's get on with it. that's what this is, me getting on with it. what it *is*, i tell my friend, finally, is finding ways to work in a language, in a form, and in a place, that does not love me, so that i might incite and experience joy and love regardless within its precincts. that joy might trouble its structural soundness, that there might be more give in the skin, more room for the world, and for all of its other others. to build a new, better, ever-more-audacious book of beasts. to celebrate us. to raise us.

BIBLIOGRAPHY OF WORKS CITED

INTRODUCTION

Mary Douglas, *Purity and Danger* (1966; Routledge, 2003).

Judith Halberstam, *The Queer Art of Failure* (Duke University Press, 2011).

ABJECT SPECTACLE / UNNATURAL LANGUAGE

Imogen Tyler, 'Chav Mum Chav Scum' in *Feminist Media Studies* (2008).

Peggy Phelan, *Unmarked: The Politics of Performance* (1993, Taylor Francis, 2003)

Rosemarie Garland-Thomson, *Freakery: Cultural Spectacles of the Extraordinary Body* (Columbia University Press, 1996). Also see *Staring: How We Look* (Columbia University Press, 2009).

Georges Bataille, 'Abjection and Miserable Forms' in *More and Less*, ed. Sylvère Lotringer, trans. Yvonne Shafir (1934; MIT Press, 1993).

Sue Donaldson and Will Kymlicka, *Zoopolis: A Political Theory of Animal Rights*, (Oxford University Press, 2011). Sarah Novak, 'Braying peasants and the poet as prophet: Gower and the people in the Vox clamantis' in *Études anglaises,* Vol. 66, no. 3 (2013).

Donna Haraway, *When Species Meet* (University of Minnesota Press, 2008).

Julia Kristeva, *Powers of Horror* (Columbia University Press, 1980).

Gayatri Chakravorty Spivak, 'Can the Subaltern Speak?' in *A Critique of Postcolonial Reason: Toward a History of the Vanishing Present* (1988; Harvard University Press, 1999).

THE FERAL WHO ARE ALWAYS WITH ME

Joyelle McSweeney, *The Necropastoral: Poetry, Media, Occults* (University of Michigan Press, 2015).

Maurice Blanchot, *The Space of Literature* (1955; University of Nebraska Press, 1982).

Mikhail Bakhtin, *Rabelais and His World*, trans. Hélène Iswolsky (Indiana University Press, 1984).

Rachel J.D. Smith, *Excessive Saints: Gender, Narrative, and Theological Invention in Thomas of Cantimpré's Mystical Hagiographies* (Columbia University Press, 2018).

China Miéville, *The Limits of Utopia* (Salvage, 2015).

Bishnupriya Ghosh, 'The Subaltern at the Edge of the Popular', in *Postcolonial Studies* 8:4 (2005).

Édouard Glissant, *Poetics of Relation* (University of Michigan Press, 1997).

Judith Butler, *Bodies that Matter: On the Discursive Limits of "sex"* (Routledge, 1993).

Josephine Donovan, *The Aesthetics of Care: On the Literary Treatment of Animals* (Bloomsbury, 2016).

Claude Cahun, *Disavowals: Or, Cancelled Confessions* (MIT Press, 2017).

Peter Harrison, 'Having Dominion: Genesis and the Mastery of Nature' in *Environmental stewardship: Critical perspectives, past and present,* ed. R. J. Berry (T & T Clark International, 2006).

Christopher de Hamel in *Book of Beasts: A Facsimile of MS. Bodley 764 (*Bodleian Library, 2008).

T. H. White, *The Book of Beasts: Being a Translation from a Latin*

Bestiary of the Twelfth Century (Dover, 1984).

Valerie Solanas, *SCUM Manifesto* (Verso, 2016).

Natasha Seegert, thesis: 'Animate Rhetoric, Queer Beasts: Rewilding Domesticity' (2014).

Leah DeVun, *The Shape of Sex: Nonbinary Gender from Genesis to the Renaissance* (Columbia University Press, 2021).

Ron Baxter, *Bestiaries and Their Users in the Middle Ages* (Sutton Publishing, 1998).

Eoin Neeson, 'Woodland in History and Culture' in *Nature in Ireland: A Scientific and Cultural History,* ed. John Wilson Foster (McGill-Queens Press, 1997).

Keith Thomas, *Man and the Natural World: Changing Attitudes in England 1500-1800* (Penguin, 1983).

Charles Kingsley, *His Letters and Memories of His Life* (Cambridge University Press, 2012).

George Yancy, *Black Bodies, White Gazes: The Continuing Significance of Race in America* (Rowman & Littlefield, 2017).

Jeanne Dubino, 'Mad Dogs and Irishmen: Dogs, Dracula, and the Colonial Irish Other' in *Animals in Irish Literature and Culture* (Palgrave Macmillan, 2014).

Henry Mayhew, *London Labour and the London Poor* (1864; Penguin Books, 1985).

Aaron M. Moe, *Zoopoetics: Animals and the Making of Poetry* (Lexington Books, 2013).

Donna Haraway, *The Companion Species Manifesto: Dogs, People, and Significant Otherness* (Prickly Paradigm Press, 2003).

Jack London, *The People of the Abyss* (1903; Pluto Press, 1991).

POUNDLAND ACADEMIC VERSUS THE RAINBOW CAPITALIST BORG

Anahid Nersessian, *The Calamity Form: On Poetry and Social Life* (University of Chicago Press, 2020).

Aimé Césaire, *Discourse on Colonialism* (1949; Monthly Review Press, 2001).

As quoted in J. Baird Callicott 'Animal Liberation: A Triangular Affair', *Environmental Ethics* 2: Issue 4 (1980)

As quoted in *Animals and Women: Feminist Theoretical Explorations*, eds. Carol J. Adams, Josephine Donovan (Duke University Press, 1995).

Maggie Hennefeld and Nicholas Sammond, eds. *Abjection Incorporated: Mediating the Politics of Pleasure and Violence* (Duke University Press, 2020).

Sianne Ngai and Lauren Berlant, 'Comedy Has Issues' in *Critical Inquiry* 43 (Winter, 2017).

Andrei Codrescu, *Bibliodeath: My Archives (With Life in Footnotes)* (Antibookclub, 2013).

Cynthia Cruz, *The Melancholia of Class: A Manifesto for the Working Class* (Repeater, 2021).

ON 'RENARDIE' (FOX PROBLEMS, FOX PIVOTS)

Silvia Federici, *Caliban and the Witch: Women, the Body and Primitive Accumulation* (Autonomedia, 2004).

Claude Lévi-Strauss, *Structural Anthropology*, trans. C. Jacobson and B. G. Schoepf (Basic Books, 1963).

John Berger, 'Why Look at Animals' in *About Looking* (Bloomsbury, 1980).

Terry O'Connor, *Animals as Neighbors: The Past and Present of Commensal Animals (The Animal Turn)* (Michigan State University Press, 2013).

Jean R. Scheidegger, *Le Roman de Renart ou le texte de la dérision* (DROZ, 1989).

Simone Weil, *First and Last Notebooks* (Wipf and Stock, 2015).

Gilles Deleuze, *Francis Bacon: The Logic of Sensation,* trans. Daniel W. Smith (Continuum, 2004).

Audre Lorde, *Cancer Journals* (1980; Penguin, 2015).

COMMUNITY & HAUNTING / THE HAUNTED COMMUNITY

Fred Moten and Stefano Harney, *The Undercommons: Fugitive Planning & Black Study* (Minor Compositions, 2013).

'Letter from Marx To his Father In Trier' in *The First Writings of Karl Marx* (Ig Pub, 2006).

Jacques Derrida, *Spectres of Marx* (Routledge, 1993).

Eyal Weizman, *Forensic Architecture Violence at the Threshold of Detectability* (Zone Books, 2017).

Avery Gordon, *Ghostly Matters: Haunting and the Sociological Imagination* (University of Minnesota Press, 1997).

Naomi Mandel, *Against the Unspeakable: Complicity, the Holocaust, and Slavery in America* (University of Virginia Press, 2006).

Theodor Adorno, 'Cultural Criticism and Society' in *Prisms* (1949; MIT Press, 1993).

Gilles Deleuze, *Essays Critical and Clinical,* trans. D.W. Smith and M. A. Greco (1949; University of Minnesota Press, 1997).

Luce Irigaray, *An Ethics of Sexual Difference* (Bloomsbury Academic, 1982).

Mary Russo, *The Female Grotesque: Risk, Excess and Modernity* (Taylor Francis, 2012).

Maria Angel and Anna Gibbs, 'At the Speed of Light: From Cyberfeminism to Xenofeminism, Cyberfeminism, Xenofeminism and the Digital Ecology of Bodies' in *#Womentechlit*, ed. María Mencía (West Virginia University Press, 2017).

Jean Paul Sartre, *Being and Nothingness* (1969; Routledge, 2022).

As quoted in *The Red Army Faction, a Documentary History Volume 1: Projectiles for the People*, J. Smith and André Moncourt eds. (PM Press, 2009).

Mary Daly, *Gyn/Ecology: The Metaethics of Radical Feminism* (Beacon Press, 1978).

Hanna Fenichel Pitkin, *The Attack of the Blob: Hannah Arendt's Concept of the Social* (University of Chicago Press, 1998).

Roland Barthes, *The Responsibility of Forms: Critical Essays on Music, Art, and Representation* (University of California Press, 1991).

See Nicholas P. Canny, *The Elizabethan Conquest of Ireland: A Pattern Established 1565-76* (New York: Barnes & Nobles, 1976), and Edmund Spenser, 'A View of the Present State of Ireland, Discourse by way of a Dialogue Between Eudoxs and Irenius', in *Elizabethan Ireland: A Selection of Writings by Elizabethan Writers on Ireland*, James P. Myers ed. (Hamden: Archon Books, 1983), and Barnabe Rich, 'A New Description of Ireland, Together with the Manners, Customs, and Dispositions of the People' in the same.

In *The English and Scottish Popular Ballads*, Mark F. Heiman and Laura Saxton Heiman eds. (Loomis House, 2008).

"ALWAYS ANGULAR, NEVER STRAIGHT"

Frederika Bain, in *Melusine's Footprint: Tracing the Legacy of a Medieval Myth*, Deva Kemmis, Melissa Ridley Elmes and Misty Urban, eds. (Brill, 2017).

Comité Invisible, *The Coming Insurrection* (Semiotexte, 2009).

Victoria Adukwei Bulley, *Quiet* (Faber and Faber, 2022).

Marie Thompson, '*Gossips, sirens, hi-fi wives: feminizing the threat of noise*' in *Resonances: Noise and Contemporary Music* (Bloomsbury, 2013).

Anne Carson, *Glass, Irony & God* (New Directions, 1992).

Jean-Marie Gleize, *Tarnac, A Preparatory Act*, Joshua Clover ed., Joshua Clover, Abigail Lang and Bonnie Roy trans. (Kenning Editions, 2014).

Hélène Cixous, 'The Laugh of the Medusa' in *The Hélène Cixous Reader* (Routledge, 2003).

Raquelle K. Bostow, 'Loving Across Borders: The Queer, Transspecies Intimacies of Cixousian Sexual Difference' in *MLN*, Vol. 134 (John Hopkins University Press, 2019).

Donna Haraway, *Staying with the Trouble: Making Kin in the Cthulucene* (Duke University Press, 2016).

'TH E SERPENT LOOKS BACK AND RETURNS'
(SNAKE EPILOGUE)

Sharon Murphy, '"Be careful. I am death!": Rikki-Tikki-Tavi and Britons' "Great War" against Snakes in Late-Nineteenth-Century India' in *Children's Literature* Vol. 50 (Johns Hopkins University Press, 2022).

M. Daphne Kutzer, *Empire's Children: Empire and Imperialism in Classic British Children's Books* (Garland, 2000).

ON 'THE NAMES OF THE HARE IN ENGLISH'

Carolynn Van Dyke, 'Names of the Beasts: Tracking the Animot in Medieval Texts' in *Studies in the Age of Chaucer*, Vol. 34 (January 2012).

Eric Savoy, 'The Signifying Rabbit' in *Narrative*, Vol. 3, No. 2 (May 1995).

Rebecca Kukla, *Mass Hysteria: Medicine, Culture, and Mothers' Bodies* (Rowman & Littlefield, 2005).

Karen Harvey, *The Imposteress Rabbit Breeder: Mary Toft and Eighteenth-Century England* (Oxford University Press, 2020).

Erica Fudge, *Brutal Reasoning: Animals, Rationality, and Humanity in Early Modern England* (Cornell University Press, 2006).

THE CABINET / THE CLOSET

Audre Lorde, 'Poetry Is Not a Luxury' in *Sister Outsider* (1985; Penguin, 2019).

Jean Baudrillard, *The System of Objects* (Verso, 1996).

Peter M. Daly, *Literature in the Light of the Emblem: Structural Parallels between the Emblem and Literature in the Sixteenth and Seventeenth Centuries* (University of Toronto Press, 1979).

Paula Findlen, *Possessing Nature: Museums, Collecting, and Scientific Culture in Early Modern Italy* (University of California Press, 1994).

Stephen T. Asma, *Stuffed Animals and Pickled Heads The Culture and Evolution of Natural History Museums* (Oxford University Press, 2003).

ACKNOWLEDGEMENTS

With thanks to the University of Cambridge, the Parker Library, and to Magma Poetry, where excerpts from this book first appeared.

Selected other titles by Out-Spoken Press